Faeriecraft

Also by Alicen & Neil Geddes-Ward

Music and Meditation CDs

Sleeve notes and illustrations for Llewellyn and Juliana,
Journey to the Fairies, New World Music, 2003

The Faerie Cottage: Guided Meditation for Relaxation and Imagination,
featuring music by Llewellyn, New World Music, 2004

***

Hay House Titles of Related Interest

Books*/Card Decks

**The Art of Wiccan Healing*, by Sally Morningstar
Ask Your Guides Oracle Cards, by Sonia Choquette
Developing Your Intuition with Magic Mirrors, by Uma Reed
**Healing with the Angels*, by Doreen Virtue, Ph.D. (also a card deck)
**Healing with the Fairies*, by Doreen Virtue, Ph.D. (also a card deck)
Magical Spells Cards, by Lucy Cavendish
The Oracle Tarot Cards, by Lucy Cavendish
*Sacred Ceremony, by Steven D. Farmer, Ph.D.
**Secrets & Mysteries of the World*, by Sylvia Browne
*Spellbinding, by Claudia Blaxell

***

All of the above are available at your local bookstore,
or may be ordered by visiting:

Hay House USA: www.hayhouse.com
Hay House Australia: www.hayhouse.com.au
Hay House UK: www.hayhouse.co.uk
Hay House South Africa: orders@psdprom.co.za

Faeriecraft

ALICEN & NEIL
GEDDES-WARD

HAY HOUSE, INC.
Carlsbad, California
London • Sydney • Johannesburg
Vancouver • Hong Kong

Published and distributed in the United States by: Hay House, Inc.,
P.O. Box 5100, Carlsbad, CA 92018-5100 • *Phone:* (760) 431-7695
or (800) 654-5126 • *Fax:* (760) 431-6948 or (800) 650-5115 •
www.hayhouse.com • *Published and distributed in Australia by:* Hay
House Australia Pty. Ltd., 18/36 Ralph St., Alexandria NSW 2015 •
Phone: 612-9669-4299 • *Fax:* 612-9669-4144 • www.hayhouse.com.
au • *Published and distributed in the United Kingdom by:* Hay House
UK, Ltd. • Unit 62, Canalot Studios • 222 Kensal Rd., London W10
5BN • *Phone:* 44-20-8962-1230 • *Fax:* 44-20-8962-1239 • www.
hayhouse.co.uk • *Published and distributed in the Republic of South
Africa by:* Hay House SA (Pty), Ltd., P.O. Box 990, Witkoppen 2068
• *Phone/Fax:* 27-11-706-6612 • orders@psdprom.co.za • *Distributed
in Canada by:* Raincoast • 9050 Shaughnessy St., Vancouver, B.C.
V6P 6E5 • *Phone:* (604) 323-7100 • *Fax:* (604) 323-2600

Design: Leanne Siu; and Scribe Design Ltd, Ashford, Kent, UK

ISBN 10: 1-4019-0610-9

08   07   06   05   4 3 2 1
1st printing, July 2005

Printed in the United States of America

Faeriecraft is dedicated to
our children
Morgan Fawn, our merfaerie
Tam Lin Alexander, our little elfin

"Faeriecraft brings us wonderful reminders of the importance of connecting with the fairies and with nature. The book is filled with excellent suggestions for working, healing, and celebrating with the fairies. The fairies are the environmentalist angels, and the more that we believe in them, the more power they have to clean up our world. It's my sincere prayer that everyone who reads Faeriecraft will go to a park or garden and get to know the fairies who live there."

— **DOREEN VIRTUE, PH.D.,** THE BEST-SELLING AUTHOR OF
HEALING WITH THE FAIRIES AND *ANGEL MEDICINE*

'Just follow the first and only rule of faeriecraft
and you will get along just fine

Rule one: Normal rules do not apply

Contents

Preface

The Indrinking Spell

'Our queen and her elves come here anon.'

WILLIAM SHAKESPEARE, A MIDSUMMER NIGHT'S DREAM

The Faerie Rite; this is how it all began.

I remember the sweetest of scents on the night air as the maiden placed a bowl of honey on our faerie altar. The tree stump at the centre of our circle was covered in moss and decorated in chains of white frothy hawthorn flowers. This was the night of Beltaine, the night when the veil to the Land of Elphame draws thin. It was to be a one-off, never to be repeated before or since, because we would enter a realm so entrancing, so captivating and all-consuming that we would never need to go there again. We knew that faeries were the inner knowing within us, the secret places that we could not reach alone. We were about to be given our words' worth.

The maiden took up the besom and as she began to sweep the circle of the woodland floor, I gasped as I saw tiny blue sparks, like electricity, flying off the broomstick. 'Spider, spider, what are you spinning? A cloak for a faerie, I'm just beginning,' the maiden sang as she swept and I could not keep my eyes from the broomstick that danced its sweeping way around our circle.

Once the circle had been prepared and cast, the Faerie Priest and I stood opposite one another. This was when I saw it: the beginning of the feeling that was never to end. We had both closed our eyes and as he invoked the Faerie King, the elfin magic that I shall never forget took us by the hands, drenching us in a star-spangled mind place. I invoked the Faerie Queen Mab and it was then that we partook of the indrinking spell of one another. We entered Faerie Land, the place of spiritual ecstasy and enrapture, where our existence and the place between the worlds kiss.

EXTRACT FROM *THE KISS OF TWO WORLDS*,
A NOVEL BY ALICEN GEDDES-WARD

Bright Blessings and Thanks to ...

We would like to thank all our very patient and delightful models who became immortalized as faeries: Gabriella Clark, Morgan Geddes-Ward, Francesca Pandolfino, Lara (Velvet) Rayburn and Chad Hall.

Special thanks go to those gifted friends who helped us at photo shoots: Dominic Williams, Rick Clark and Claire Bond.

Thank you also to Llewellyn and Juliana for their inspiration and encouragement in everything creative that we do and, most importantly, for always believing in us.

To Becky Bunsic, our number one fan.

Indebted thanks also to Josie Marsden, who spent a lot of time she didn't have with us and our preliminary manuscript, scouring it for mistakes, knowing that she would get absolutely nothing in return. Our unseen angel.

Special gratitude must go to Merlyn and Epona of the Children of Artemis organization for their belief and untiring support for us over the years.

With love and thanks to all the members of Grimalkin for their support and patience.

Chapter 10, 'The Faerie Ring', is dedicated to our friends in Grimalkin. Without your inspiration it would not have been written.

Thank you to Michelle Pilley, Jo Lal, Megan Slyfield, Leanne Siu and Giovanna Ceroni at Hay House, for shaping our dream. Our gratitude to Lizzie Hutchins for her patience and perseverance.

Thank you to Morgan for allowing us to use her inspirational King and Queen of Cobwebs.

Thank you to our faerie helpers, who are really the ones behind this book, inspiring and guiding us, making the creating of this book a truly magical experience.

Thanks to both our parents and families for their support over the years and invaluable babysitting skills!

Chapter 7, 'Away with the Faeries', is dedicated to Neil's dear friend, the late Steve Saunders.

Thanks to Jack Gale, our mortal Jack Frost, for help in the making of this book as well as the magical pathway trodden in snow.

Thanks to Lisa and Jim Bennett and Towse Harrison for their input in the original versions of 'The Naming of a Faerie Childe'.

The authors also wish to thank everyone who gave permission to reproduce the quotes in this book:

Steve Fox, *The Faerie Ring*, 1998, www.gothicangel.co.uk

Brian Froud and Terry Jones, *Lady Cottington's Pressed Fairy Book*, Pavilion, London, 2000

Doreen Valiente, *An ABC of Witchcraft Past and Present*, Robert Hale, London, 1973

Dominic Williams, 'The Faerie Temptress', unpublished

Every effort has been made to contact the copyright holders, but in the event that an oversight has occurred, we will be delighted to rectify any omissions in future editions of this book.

1

Into the Faerie Mound

Who Are the Faeries?

'I serve the fairy queen,
To dew her orbs upon the green;
The cowslips tall her pensioners be;
In their gold coats spots you see;
There be rubies, fairy favours,
In those freckles live their savours:
I must go seek some dew-drops here
And hang a pearl in every cowslip's ear.'

WILLIAM SHAKESPEARE,
A MIDSUMMER NIGHT'S DREAM

What Is Faeriecraft?

The first line from Shakespeare's quotation, 'I serve the fairy queen', invokes entrancing images and feelings for me. If I had to sum up in a sentence exactly what faeriecraft meant to me, then it would be precisely that: to serve the Faerie Queen. For indeed the Faerie Queen and her kingdom have an inspiring vision for us to follow. They are waiting for us to build a divine relationship with them so that our consciousness and that of the planet can unfold in radiance and beauty. Within these pages I am going to share with you the sacred and all-encompassing way in which the faeries have been working with me and how you can walk this pathway too.

Faeriecraft is essentially the merging of the faerie faith and the practice of witchcraft or wicca. Witchcraft is also known as the Old Religion and has its roots in paganism, the traditional faith of the ancient peoples of our land. Paganism is everyone's spiritual heritage and works with nature and nature spirits. Out of this come the faeries: a natural honouring of everything about you. Sadly, in our mainstream culture, faeries are generally perceived to be a fancy that only children believe in. Yet awareness of faeries and their sacred nature is growing, and we are now at a point where their spiritual presence is unfurling in our consciousness. The time has now come for faeriecraft to emerge. Faeriecraft is an ancient pathway and is still practised today by groups and individuals. It seems to be a 20th/21st-century occurrence that certain individuals carve a variant pathway of faeriecraft for others to follow and become initiated into. There is the feri tradition of Victor Anderson, the Faerie Tradition and Third Road of Francesca De Grandis, Faerie Wicca according to Kisma K. Stepanich and the Welsh Faerie Craft of the Tribe of Dynion Mwyn, to name but a few.

Two summers ago I was at a conference, sitting in the Green Room waiting to be called to conduct my talk. With me were several other speakers, all waiting to start their respective workshops and talks. We were all making polite conversation to pass the time. A Scottish speaker, whom I had previously met only briefly, asked me, 'And what is your talk about?' I answered that it was about faeriecraft and he replied, 'Faeriecraft according to whom?' This was when I realized that the faeriecraft I was living and presenting did not belong to any of the aforementioned faerie authors and gurus and had a very different slant from that of those who had gone before me.

The faeriecraft I am introducing to you allows *anyone* to follow its sparkling pathway without a teacher, guru or group. I do believe that the faeries are for everyone. They really do dwell in every hanging dewdrop, every intricate snowflake and glistening delicate spider's web. This is my version of faeriecraft, the pathway as I have shaped it, a meeting of my own ideas, research and the influences and information that have been given to me by the faeries themselves. It is more *faerie centred* than any other pathway that I know. It allows those who are not from a wiccan background to find a way into this system, as although faeriecraft is a melding of the faerie faith and wicca. I am simply using the wiccan framework to hang the folds of faeriecraft upon. This form of faeriecraft really works well because it begins with the imagination and faeries, and everyone has an experience of faeries, however simplistic, from fairy stories as children. This faerie-centred pathway is the way that I shape my life and that of my family. Through this book I will gently guide you through faeriecraft, sharing with you the things that I do and why they work well for me.

About the Faeries' Vision

Faeriecraft is a step to working consciously with the fey. The faerie realm is a very special aspect of the divine that we are allowed to work with. One reason why the faeries wish to work more closely with humans at the present time is the jeopardy of our planet. All the inhabitants of the faerie realm are the living consciousness of the earth; they are the breeze on your face, the sand between your toes, the trickling water running down your gutter after rainfall and the flame at your candlelit dinner. As sacred custodians of all aspects of nature, faeries know that our environment has an intelligent and spiritual consciousness.

Faeriecraft looks at nature more closely and appreciates its beauty. Noticing the small things is the window to Faerie Land. I have a very tiny garden, but even there the faeries dwell. I am constantly being surprised by the Otherworld of nature and where it can take me. While walking down the short pathway in my garden, I had to stop abruptly in my tracks. On a bush of heavy white roses was a spider's web, suspended by the flowers, with the spider repairing its gossamer home. I felt an impulse to pause and peer at this sight, which was very ordinary, but at that moment it seemed potently magical and something sparked in my imagination. We are often too busy to stop and look at the little things in life, but at that moment I did pause, and I knew that I was peering through the magic mirror of Faerie Land. The faeries, in their way, were reminding me to look.

Small moments in nature can entrance and suddenly take you out of your everyday world into another place, another time. Nature is on the cusp of Faerie Land, melding our two worlds together. Open your heart to the possibilities of magic and it will find you and, like the faeries, always surprise you. Your life may never be quite the same again once you permit the faeries to touch your existence.

The ultimate aim of this book is for you to emerge inspired to work further with the faeries and with the knowledge and confidence to call yourself a Faerie Priest or Priestess. Faeriecraft does not require you to be initiated by yourself or anyone else. I have found that the faeries themselves will initiate you in a way that is right for you. A knowledge of witchcraft or wicca is not essential to practise the faeries' pathway, as I believe that faeriecraft is simply a natural expression of the magic that we all first experienced as children. The simple elements of witchcraft which are woven into the path of faerie are all explained in this book.

There is a very good reason why faeries and witchcraft are placed together as a magical practice, and it is useful to know the connection. Throughout history the relationship between the faerie race and the witch has been one of mutual respect. Faeries have long been known to help witches out when they are in need, and it would seem that the witch has a natural propensity towards the realms where faeries dwell, living a life with one foot in this world and the other foot in the place between the worlds. In Doreen Valiente's classic work *The ABC of Witchcraft Past and Present*, she comments that 'the relationship between the world of witchcraft and the faerie has always been close; so close, indeed, that it is not easy to draw a precise boundary in these enchanted lands, and to say where one world ends and another begins'. So faeriecraft is a natural extension of the original witch's pathway, although it now has so many elements that are unique that it largely transcends witchcraft and introduces faeries as being a devotional journey in their own right.

Faeries also favour sensitive people as well as witches, as one such documented case illustrates. In *A Book of Fairies* Katherine Briggs recounts the story of Anne Jeffries: '....in 1645 she fell into a fit, and was ill after it for some time, but when she recovered she declared that she had been carried away by the faeries...' So well known was her relationship with the faerie people that 'she was arrested in 1646 at the suit of John Tregeagle...' He committed her to prison and gave orders that she was not to be fed. By 1647 she had still not been fed at all, but was reported to be in good health, made no complaints and was thus released. It was said that the faeries had taken her food all the while she had been detained.

Another well-known story is of how the Rollright Stones in Oxfordshire came to be. The witch involved here was said to have given her faerie friends an offering of the finest milk. In return they assisted her in turning the invading enemy to stone.

These are the tales that legends are made of, but in this book we turn our attention to the real-life relationship between the faeries and a modern faerie seeker. Honouring the faeries is a life pathway, a spiritual journey that should not be taken lightly and can relate to every aspect of our lives. Faeriecraft is intrinsically the yearning to nurture a relationship with the faeries and work harmoniously with them. This means on all levels, for the natural world and for humanity. It means not harming others, including yourself, and living with respect in our environment. The faerie kingdoms live without law, and all those who dwell there abide by the code of self-responsibility. This is their ultimate vision for the human race, although we would be the first to admit that we are a long way from it at the moment.

Faeries are also God's messengers through the magical consciousness of our living planet. They are there to remind us of our relationship to nature. The Earth is a reflection of our spiritual, emotional and physical well-being. If we are in discord, then much of our environment will be in this state too.

Working on every level with nature brings us back to ourselves and feeds our souls. I am not saying that you have to have a love of gardening; you may simply appreciate nature by taking a long walk in your local park or woods, growing herbs on your windowsill to use in cooking or meditating on the sounds of the sea. But building a relationship with nature also builds a bridge to Faerie Land and raises your spiritual vibrations.

Focusing on the four elements can also bring you back in touch with nature. This can be done in the simplest ways; for example, lighting a candle at mealtimes instead of switching on the electric light, or putting your washing on the line to dry instead of stuffing it into the tumble dryer. Even drying your clothes by the natural breeze, instead of electricity, is a small magical act. You are making a conscious decision to experience the elements.

The faeries are not difficult to find, as they are all around us in nature. We just need to look a bit harder. Once we decide to seek them, they will be there to greet us and illuminate our lives. My own way of feeling the connection to the element of fire is to collect dead wood from the forest floor for use on my open fire. Once when I lifted up a small log to throw it in the wheelbarrow, a woody-coloured frog leaped out. He then stayed still long enough for our children to see the beautiful patterns on his back for camouflage among the dead leaves and bark. If I had just switched on the central heating, we would not have had this precious experience. To sit tucked up in an armchair in the evening, feeling the heat of the fire on my cheeks and watching the mesmerizing flames, reminds me of my connection to nature.

It is very easy for us all to live divorced from nature, but to work successfully with the faeries we do need to make some concessions in our lives to let nature in once more. If you do not give yourself the opportunity to see a frog once in a while, how will you ever get the chance to see a faerie?

Who Are the Faeries?

Faerie is a general term and is interchangeable with *elf* in all its variants, as a name to describe all the beings who dwell in Faerie Land. The faeries are known to be divided into four distinct groups, which are:

Enchanters and Enchantresses

These are sometimes known as Tempters and Temptresses, and I have renamed them as Faerie Priests and Priestesses. They are human beings who are aligned to the faerie race by way of their destiny, faerie ambassadors in the human world who have been bestowed with psychic or empathic gifts by the faeries. They are believed to rest in Faerie Land after their death, and in life they are sensitive, creative people who invariably learn the arts of magic at some time during their lives.

Creatures and Demons

These are also thought to be aligned to the faerie race, and some have a magical connection to faeries. These include a wide spectrum of beasts such as unicorns, centaurs, trolls, the Loch Ness Monster, urchins and dragons. These creatures display characteristics ranging from the innately spiritual, beautiful and benevolent to the downright nasty.

The Elemental Faeries

These are the spirits of nature which dwell in every living thing upon the Earth. They are the sylphs of air, the undines of water, the salamanders of fire and the gnomes of earth.

The Faerie or Elfin People

These are a race of magical beings who dwell in subterranean mounds, rocks or faerie islands that are shrouded from view underwater. They are said to be invisible and silent most of the time, unless they choose otherwise. They live in organized societies governed by Kings and Queens presiding in faerie courts. The faerie race is divided into two types of fey. One type is the Trooping Faeries, who are the aristocracy, so-called because they travel in processional form and are believed to be descendants of ancient demoted pagan gods. The second is the solitary faeries, who are of a wilder nature than their Trooping cousins and are the peasantry beings of Faerie Land.

The Elemental Faeries

Faeries are the intrinsic inhabitants of nature and thus reflect the natural world in their appearance, culture and personality. They are a race of fully sentient beings with feelings and rights similar to our own. They dwell in natural places such as trees, root systems, gushing streams and woodland groves to name but a few.

All elemental faeries belong to either air, fire, water or earth. There are thousands of different types of faeries all belonging to many countries and cultures, but they will always be related to one of the four elements. Occasionally there is an elemental that does not easily sit in a category. For example, I encountered an electricity elemental when our woodland ritual site happened to be in close proximity to an electricity pylon. These beings would belong to the element of fire, and there are many modern elementals who need some thought as to which sphere of nature they belong.

The sixteenth-century alchemist, doctor and philosopher Paracelsus gave the faeries of the four elements the names that we still use today. The sylphs or sylvestres are the faeries of air, the salamanders or newts are the fire feys, the undines or nymphs are the water faeries and the gnomes or gnomus are the earth-dwelling faeries. It is important to become familiar with these types of faeries, so that you can address them properly and work with them on a deeper level.

The Winged Sylphs

These are the elementals of air, and their name derives from the Greek *silphe*, meaning 'butterfly' or 'moth'. This is because the vast majority of sylph-categorized faeries have some sort of wings, although these are not the wings of the three-dimensional kind that we are accustomed to.

The sylphs represent all the attributes of the element of air in real terms and symbolic terms. They are as light as a feather, quick and flighty, and represent freedom of the spirit, thought and emotion. They are the celestial messengers from this dimension to the place between the worlds where dreams and the experiences of the inner life dwell. They are mutable faeries, able to shapeshift to suit their environment, their mood or the expectations of the company they keep. They please themselves, and their fluid form allows them to transcend physical reality. The form they take is merely an assumption we have of the way in which they appear to us. They are generally believed to be very small and transparent, and they are frequently seen surrounded by their own personal aura of light. Sometimes their bodies appear to be made up of light too.

The sylph faeries have an affinity with birds, and there are many legends of women turning into birds and vice versa. Some sylphs take on the form of birds or some of the features of birds. They may have feathered wings, for example, or may have a human body and a bird's head. They have also been known to inhabit birds' nests or create faerie nests of their own. They help as guardians of eggs, sometimes sleeping in nests too.

Sylph faeries in their conventional form and in the form of birds are very often messengers from the Otherworld. They bring us messages from our souls that we cannot uncover ourselves. They are the spiritual couriers for our unseen selves, bringing into the light that which is buried within ourselves and those around us.

If you would like to visualize a sylph, you may be inspired by the imagery captured in the following words:

Imagine a garden in the autumn. A little girl is there, dressed in a woolly hat and coat. There is a blackbird sitting on the fence whistling its morning song. The little girl calls to the blackbird, whom she visits every morning before she goes to school. The blackbird is singing as if to her, watching her from the fence with an extraordinary knowing look in his eye. The little girl has a small piece of folded paper in her hands, which she holds up as if to show the blackbird.

Her mother's voice calls from inside the house, telling her that it is time for her to get ready to go to school. She puts the little letter she has written to her blackbird friend under a heavy stone, then she runs inside.

When the blackbird is sure that the little girl is inside the house, he hops down from the fence, landing on the large stone. His wings begin to shimmer with a green light which then surrounds his whole body. The beautiful sleek black feathers on his body transform into feathered garments draping a faerie form. The sylph boy looks an enchanting creature with his slanting green eyes and long black hair. His shoes are lined with feather down and his trousers and jacket are the green-black of a blackbird's sheen. He tugs the letter out from underneath the stone and tucks it in his black jewelled crown. He pulls out a feather from his wings and leaves it under the stone for the little girl to find. He raises his wings to their full span and all at once he is encircled by a whirl of green light. He takes flight to a nearby tree and there he stands on the edge of a blackbird's nest and takes the letter from under his crown. He places the precious letter in the nest, among the moss and down, as if it is a piece of treasure.

The Entrancing Salamanders

Salamanders are the spirits of fire. They inhabit every flame and soar and dance through the air as sparks and streaks of light in hues of red, orange and gold. They reside in all forms of fire, including energy associated with the sun. These faeries have the least form of all the elemental beings, as their energy is so transient and transmutable. They are quick and unpredictable, making them the elementals which are most respected for their dangerous qualities. They also possess the ability to hypnotize and bring people to the Otherworlds by entrancing them. They are both magical and sacred, hazardous and revered.

The salamanders are symbolic of your own life force, of passionate feelings, the spark of ideas and creativity, the spirit of aliveness and the kick you get from doing something on impulse.

Traditionally, the hearth was a place that was treated with great respect in every home. Many people believed in the faerie in the hearth and periodically left gifts out for them. There are many tales of hearth faeries who have felt neglected and taken mischievous revenge on their house-holders.

In appearance salamanders are very like the element that they represent, ranging from beings resembling tapered flames and sparks to faeries with flaming hair and personalities to match.

Try visualizing on this salamander word picture:

An old woman sits before her fireplace in a velvet armchair. She is so close to the fire that her slippered feet are almost touching the hearth. But she feels the cold, and evenings by the fireside knitting are her favourite form of comfort. Her contented tabby cat sits upon the arm of the chair and purrs contentedly at the all-encompassing heat that emanates from the fireplace.

The wood spits and crackles from within the flames as the fire gently roars. The coals glint and gleam with red heat and periodically tiny sparks from the dry wood flit from the flames onto the hearth tiles. The old woman gradually knits more slowly, until finally her hands rest motionless on her lap. The soporific gentle heat has lulled her to sleep. She falls willingly into dreams, while the cat is mesmerized by the flickering flames.

As the cat watches the blaze, entranced, the flames begin to take a shape and look like long golden curls and wisps belonging to raptures of fiery-coloured hair. Through the centre of the flaming locks slowly emerges the mischievous face of a captivating young girl. She throws her head back and appears to be totally absorbed by her own being. She has a warm and loving feeling radiating from her. She peers out at the cat, who is mildly interested in her appearance. She blows a kiss to him and as she does so, several sparks spit from the coals onto the hearth. When the cat receives the salamander kiss his eyelids become heavy and eventually he too succumbs to the blissful warm sleep that the old lady rests in.

With no one to add more logs to the fire, it slowly dies down. The salamander's hair becomes less ravishing as the fire diminishes to a flameless heat of hot coals, twinkling red stars into the room. The salamander rests her head on the coals and closes her eyes, preparing herself to be reborn from the ashes tomorrow.

The Beguiling Undines

The water elementals fall into two distinct sections: freshwater elementals who dwell inland and saltwater elementals who inhabit the seas and oceans.

The freshwater elementals are known as undines. They are generally portrayed as female in art and literature. Though their male counterparts do exist, they are rarer.

Undines are the Faerie Priests and Priestesses of water, the spirits and guardians of wells, lakes, trickling streams and natural springs. Their element governs the emotions and feelings that run deep within us. Water also holds connections and gateways to the Otherworlds. Although when you look into water it reflects earthly reality, beneath the surface is another place of an entirely different quality. Water is the magic looking-glass into Faerie Land, both symbolically and actually. Walking through or crossing running water is said to be a way of entering the faerie Otherworld.

As with all elementals, undines should be treated with respect, for they reflect the facets of their element. One moment a lake can be a beautiful place, reflecting the sun's rays and bringing a sense of peacefulness, and in another moment it can be responsible for injury or even death. Just as water should be respected, so should the undines, and it is wise to show some degree of caution. However, this does not mean that you should never work with them, as they can lead you on journeys to illuminate the inner self and can reflect your emotions so that you can see them more clearly.

An undine's appearance is traditionally that of a beautiful and alluring young woman resembling a female human in every way. Undines are very often exquisitely beautiful, so much so that in myth and legend mortal men have a hard time resisting their beckoning advances. They have extremely long, luxuriant hair and many sing so finely that it is a perfect sound, unsurpassed by any mortal.

The saltwater elementals are most known for their merpeople. Mermaids are the female faeries of the sea kingdoms; they are the magic in the waves and the whispering in a seashell. They keep beneath the tides the hidden enchantment which most humans have ceased to believe in.

The appearance of a mermaid is of course legendary, with the upper body of a bewitching and nubile young woman, usually with extremely long hair. Her legs are replaced by the tail of a fish. The most common image of a mermaid is perched on a rock, brushing her beautiful long hair.

There are many seafaring legends of mermaids. Some are said to have saved the lives of sailors from stormy seas, whereas others have summoned storms to cause a shipwreck. Like the undines, they have exquisite singing voices and lure mortal men to be their lovers. Some have been known to marry human lovers and bear their children, although they always yearn for the sea and some do eventually return, with or without their human husbands.

Sea elementals take many other forms apart from mermaids, including the selkies, who are the seal people, the merrows, who are the Irish sea people, the kelpies, who are the water horses, and the morgans of Cornwall and Brittany, who are the alluring sea people. All sea elementals demand the same respect as the element of water and are a privilege to work with.

If you wish to visualize an undine, you may like to begin here:

A young woman with long dark hair is sitting by the loveliest well she has ever come by. In fact she comes here whenever she can get away. If you could see the well, you would know why. It is in a lonely lush woodland and is made from stones, now covered in moss and lichen. The young woman is not the only one to have discovered the well, for it is believed to be a sacred place, associated with the goddess. Today around the walls, visitors have placed sprigs of primroses, feathers, stones, seashells, bunches of herbs and ribbons, all in honour of the goddess and the spirit of the well.

The young woman does not know why she is drawn here and why she feels a sense of peace when she visits. She could not tell you the reason why she has come here on a drizzly day, the air smelling of wet ferns and damp moss. As she sits beside the well she places her own bunch of primroses with the other offerings. She takes a deep breath and instantly feels at peace with her verdant surroundings and in turn with her inner self. She feels the breeze running through her waist-length hair and thinks for a split-second that she hears a woman singing on that breeze. She wonders if someone else is coming to visit the well. She listens for the singing again, but only hears the sounds of the woodland. She drops a primrose petal into the well water and watches the ripples spread across the sun-speckled water. When the ripples have ebbed away she looks down at her own reflection.

In the well water she sees a beautiful young woman with waist-length dark hair. She smiles when she smiles, she blinks when she blinks, so she thinks it must be her reflection. And yet there is something different today. She drops another petal into the water and the reflection ripples. She whispers her goodbyes to the well and starts to make her way back home, down the public footpath. She ponders on her reflection, not knowing why she is dwelling upon the image. Until she realizes one thing: her undine reflection was naked, whereas she had peered into the well fully clothed. The reflection could not have been her.

The Wise Gnomes

These are the elementals of the earth, and that means all forms of earth: caves, crystals and gems; the roots of trees and the sand on the beach. We all know the figure of the domestic garden gnome, looking after the earth. This popular image of the gnome is in keeping with their characters, as they are generally perceived to be the wise guardians of the earth.

As with the other elemental beings, the gnomes reflect the element to which they belong. As the earth is old and deeply wise, so are the gnomes. They are believed to live for a thousand years, reaching adulthood at the age of a hundred. Their form is well known, that of small bearded old men in red caps and stout boots. Female gnomes do exist, but they are not quite as common as the males.

There are also many other faeries who belong to the element of earth. The brownies, pixies and goblins who dwell in the intricate root systems of the earth have similar traits to the gnomes, but are mischievous and tricky in nature, unlike the dependable gnomes. Earth elementals such as the knockers are also 'changeful' in nature. These dwell in mines, particularly in Cornwall, and are extremely respected by miners. They are so called because they knock warnings at times of danger in the mines.

Here is a gnome visualization to help you focus your imagination on the earth element:

A little boy is walking in the woods in winter with his parents and he has brought with him a present for the faeries. At his favourite tree he stops and places a tiny piece of cake in a hidden nook within the roots. He stays a while talking to the faeries that he knows live in the beautiful old gnarly tree. He also leaves a sparkling stone from his garden that he has found and polished.

At last his parents call him, as they are walking deeper into the woods. The little boy reluctantly says farewell to the faeries and hurries on to his parents. Once he is certain the boy has gone, a white-bearded gnome pokes his head out from around a root. He has been there all the time, in fact his boots have been sticking out of a hole in between two crossing roots, but they have been very well camouflaged. He takes the cake and scatters it around the roots of the tree for the squirrels and birds. He then picks up the stone and smiles and places it in his waistcoat pocket. A shrew comes to sit next to him and he strokes it as if it were a cat. He seats himself on a mossy part of the tree and takes out some knitting from his jacket pocket. He is knitting himself a pair of socks and methodically knits with the shrew curled up at his feet. He smiles as he knits and a purple light glows around his waistcoat where the stone lies in his pocket.

The Kingdom of Faerie

Every country and sometimes region has its own race of faeries, each with its own hierarchy, peculiarities, customs and legends. Faeries live alongside humans, in many cases mirroring our societies' professions, family structure, crafts, communities and affairs of the heart, only on a higher spiritual level and with magical powers.

One facet of the faerie kingdom is in Ireland, where the 'good people', as they are often referred to there, are still respected in family customs and folklore today. In pagan times the people of Ireland were divided into two races: the visible race of the Celts and the invisible race of the Sidhe ('Shee'), such was the presence and prominence of the faeries. According to Irish legend a race of the Sidhe, the Tuatha de Danaan (pronounced 'too-ha day dan-an'), was forced to the Hollow Hills, the Land of Tir na nog ('teer na nogue') ('the Land of Eternal Youth'), by the Milesian peoples. They still dwell there today at the court of the Faerie King Finvarra and his Queen Oonagh.

Faerie Land

There are many myths and legends surrounding the whereabouts of Faerie Land, the place of magic and enchantment. The entrances to Faerie Land are also shrouded in mystery. Whatever the claims about the Land of Elphame, the truth is that they are all correct. The reason for this is that Elfland is an Otherwordly place, which means that it can and does exist anywhere and everywhere and has no constant geographical location in our three-dimensional world.

Many are the faerie portals or doorways, such as Glastonbury Tor in Somerset, England, and Knockshegouna, the Faerie Mound of Oonagh, east of Lough Derg in Co. Donegal, regarded as the most sacred lake in Ireland. Britain and Ireland do seem to have more than their fair share of magical faerie doorways, although all countries do of course have their own faerie traditions and culture. Faerie portals take us somewhere ethereal and not into a *real* place within the earth. They are merely energy points on the Earth that have a strong enough resonance with the divine elements to create that kind of phenomenon. I see them as the chakras of the Earth.

You do not even have to visit Elfland in person, for it is perfectly possible to visualize yourself there. It is also workable to create a faerie portal yourself, and the easiest method of achieving this is through ritual. This is explained in detail in Chapter 10, 'The Faerie Ring'.

Faerie

For clarity and simplicity, the definition of the word *faerie* in this book encompasses all those who dwell in the realm of faerie. The inhabitants of Faerie Land are so numerous and varied that all faerie beings and nature elementals, for the purpose of definition, will come under this heading. I do recognize that a mermaid, bogle or Cornish knocker do not conjure up the image of a traditional winged, sylph-like faerie. But to move forward with this book (and the faeries themselves think that it is a particularly good joke that they cannot be properly defined), we need a working definition, and *faerie* it is.

The word *fairy* derives from the old French *faerie*, which means 'enchantment'. My spelling of *faerie* here is generally recognized at the present time to be the spelling used when referring to the serious study of elemental, magical beings. Other spellings, such as *fairy*, usually refer to a kind of imaginary fairy in a trivial or childlike sense. Indeed the spellings of *faerie* are many and include *faery, fairy, faerie, fairye, fayerye, feri, frairie,* etc. My spelling of *faerie* is also dictated by the period of history that we live in and fashion. The word *elf* used to mean now what we term as *faerie*. As fashions in language change, so do our perceptions and names for the Little Folk.

Gossamer Wings and Honey Glue

Finding Your Own Way to Faerie Land

'Aug 10th 1896.
I new ther was feareys behind the potting shed.
So I went and sat very still...
the faereys was curious and inkwicitf and they all
came round to look at me...'

TERRY JONES AND BRIAN FROUD,
LADY COTTINGTON'S PRESSED FAIRY BOOK

The Way to Faerie Land

There are as many different pathways to faeriecraft as there are people. This is because it allows you to arrive at the faeries' pathway by your own personal route. The faerie way is all about your individual relationship to the fey and the particular aspect of their world that you are drawn to. The faeries will come to you in the way that is appropriate for you and you only. For example, if you are drawn to working with the environment or crystal healing, then it may be the earthly gnomes who touch you first. If you spend a lot of time in your garden and enjoy flowers, then it may be the sylph faeries who may initiate contact or reach you through your dreams or meditations.

There are also many levels on which you can experience faerie contact. Seeing a faerie must be the rarest form. The fey are much more likely to come to you through creative inspirations, intuitive feelings, experiences of the spiritual aspect of nature, meditation, dreams, visualization and also feeling touched by them through art or literature. I never actually saw a faerie as a child, I first began to see them as an adult. The artwork of Mabel Lucie Attwell in a book I owned was my first experience of faeries of any kind, and I vividly remember being totally absorbed by them. I was completely fascinated by the pictures, and they formed a faerie world inside my mind. This just goes to show that if you didn't experience actual faeries as a child (the time when it's generally accepted fey contact begins and then is later lost), it's never too late. My own faerie experiences began when I started to develop spiritually and explore my psychic senses.

On the few occasions that I have seen a faerie, it has always been in my bedroom when I have been trying to go to sleep. Beautiful lights appear and the room takes on a magical quality, as if time does not exist or has slowed down. The faeries that I have seen have always sailed past me with enormous grins, as if to say, 'Look, here's a faerie, I'm right here before your face.' It always seems to me as if they are having a great joke.

The first time I saw a faerie, it was as if I was in a trance watching her glide past me, and the room had a dreamlike atmosphere. I was mesmerized until I suddenly remembered that my husband, Neil, would absolutely love to see a faerie too. I shouted, 'Oh my God, it's a faerie in the bedroom!' Of course he woke up immediately, but on my words the faerie had disappeared completely, as if I had broken her spell. Needless to say, her grin was the last thing to fade away. The joke was on me then, for as soon as Neil woke up, there wasn't a faerie left, or even a puff of a faerie.

Surprisingly, Neil still believes in faeries, even though every time I see one the same thing happens and it disappears before he opens his eyes. Some people seem to be too earthed and may never have a faerie sighting. But of course, the faeries can touch your life in many other magical ways.

Who Are the Faerie Seekers?

Those of you reading this book may have come from a myriad of different routes. You could be someone who already has a little knowledge of meditating, visualization and so on. You may be someone who has simply picked up this book because you are fascinated by faeries and want to learn more. Whatever route you have taken to come to this book, from the complete novice to the experienced wiccan who has already dipped their toes into faeriecraft, is fine, for there are many pathways to Faerie Land, each of them as valid as the next. I have written *Faeriecraft* from a beginner's point of view, so that everything is explained in a simple step-by-step approach. However, wiccans should also find it informative, as many themes presented here put a fey slant onto those familiar wiccan ways.

Faeriecraft can also sit alongside an existing spiritual pathway that may have supported you all your life. Many people combine their faeriecraft with an established faith such as Christianity or Judaism, for instance. Faeriecraft does not have to be exclusive, as long as you are comfortable with that, as it has no dogma or doctrinal system. That would go against everything that the faeries are and has no place in faeriecraft.

How to Use This Book

For the experienced magical practitioner, dipping in and out of this book for inspiration can be recommended. However, if you are new to either working with magic or the faerie realms, it is wise to follow the book chapter by chapter and use it as a workbook. The reason for this is that working with faeries is not always straightforward, and their ways and customs are very different from our own. It is very easy to offend a faerie or work with those who do not have your best interests in mind. They are a complicated race of beings, and building a relationship with them involves enormous respect and some understanding of their lore.

Magic is also a craft which needs to be learned and its guidelines respected for your own safety. Even the most naturally gifted Faerie Priest or Priestess should follow guidelines for their magical and psychic protection. In fact the more psychically talented you are, the more careful you have to be, as you are more open and sensitive to unwelcome energies.

This book is not intended to be a dictionary or encyclopaedia of faeries, as there are already some excellent books on this subject which you can use as a resource *(see Recommended Reading)*. *Faeriecraft* is intended as a guidebook for you to begin your pathway to working with the faerie realms and to inspire you to delve deeper into faeriecraft with confidence.

My Own Pathway to Faeriecraft

In April 1988 I encountered a profound experience, one that I shall always remember with clarity. I was sleeping extremely deeply and I *dreamed* that I was taken from my bed by Queen Mab, the Faerie Queen. She held out her hand to me and I took it without thinking. This is known as a visitation dream. The place I found myself in was a meadow near my house where I had worked magically a few years previously. I could feel the breeze on my face and smell the daisies and buttercups that grew in the meadow. Queen Mab was the most enchanting creature I had ever set eyes upon. She led me to a mound in the centre of the moonlit meadow that I had hardly noticed when I had been there before. There was an opening in the grassy mound and a light, akin to lunar light, shone from the entrance.

At the entrance to the mound, Queen Mab taught me a rhyme of the most beautiful poetry I had ever heard. She then turned towards the moon-shining entrance and walked into the mound, disappearing from sight.

For a few moments I stood at the faerie portal, wondering what I was supposed to be doing. I knew instinctively that I should not follow the Faerie Queen into the mound. It soon became clear what my task was, as through the course of the night many seekers came to ask the rhyme that only I seemed to know. Once I had told them the rhyme and they could recite it back to me, they could enter the faerie mound and thus pass into the faerie realms. This began a steady stream of visitors who all needed the rhyme to enter. I recognized none of them; most of them were in their bedclothes or naked, and a couple of them wore robes. I must have admitted 30 or more people into the knoll that night, but not one single person came out.

As I began to spy the first rays of dawn trickle in through the trees that stood at the edge of the meadow, strangely while still within the visitation dream, I awoke. I then realized that I was no longer in my body and I was astral travelling. It was an ecstatic sensation to be free from my earthly body, and the reality I was in had a different non-linear quality about it. The air was like velvet, textured and deep, and I felt perfectly contented and at peace. I felt a perfect being.

As I glided through my house, it was full of faeries who must have been living there all the time, but of course I was ordinarily unaware of them. On entering my bedroom, I saw my body lying in bed, and I knew that was where I was heading. My chakras were lit up, and my solar plexus looked like an inverted cyclone, a sort of white/grey sparkling vortex that sucked me into it automatically. Entering my body was exhilarating, and as soon as I arrived back something very definite clicked within me and I opened my eyes. My bedroom appeared strange for a few moments and the absence of faeries also seemed odd. I will always remember that magical experience and believe it to be my faerie initiation.

So make space in your dreams, for the faeries are sure to visit you.

Incidentally, when I came back into my body and woke up, the first thing I tried to do was to remember the pass-rhyme that Queen Mab had taught me. I could not remember it, not even one word, and to this day I have no recollection of the rhyme I had recited all night. It was as if it had been wiped from my memory.

Queen Mab has long been my spiritual guide and helper. I have gone to her when I have experienced the lowest points in my life, and if I go to her with a question, she has never failed me yet with an answer.

My fascination with faeries had begun, as with most people, when I was a small child. As an older child my parents had called me into their bedroom and, with no ceremony, announced that faeries absolutely did not exist. To prove this fact, I was asked to stand on the bed and look at the small shelf that ran the length of their two fitted double wardrobes. There, in a perfect neat line, was every single milk tooth that had come from me and my two siblings. My parents were now officially the tooth fairy, and I did not take the news too well. I could not argue with it, of course, as the evidence was staring me in the face. The humble tooth fairy may have been a myth, but I could not believe that other faeries, the sort that danced in the woods on moonlit nights, did not exist either. I just knew deep inside that my strong belief had within it a truth. This felt immensely important at the time. Although I had never seen a faerie then, I based my existence on my belief in something in the unseen.

As a teenager my faerie experiences really began to accelerate, and people who hardly knew me called me very *fey* and seemed to acknowledge the fact, which I barely knew at the time, that faeries were drawn to me and I to them.

My faerie pathway began at a Spiritualist development circle, where I was training in mediumship, quite by accident. Although I had my fair share of deceased relatives and guides come through, I was also making a name for myself with my faerie contacts. There used to be an elf who would tug my clothes and generally make mischief during the course of the circle. Several of the other developing mediums also saw him, always next to me. I always felt that my chair in the circle was surrounded by faeries, and others in the group saw them from time to time too.

Following on, in my early twenties I began to explore witchcraft and joined a Dianic coven. I then went on to form my own coven and become a high priestess. It was in my coven that the faeries really impressed themselves upon me with their message. I always felt that I was not just a straightforward witch but a 'faeriewitch'.

Now I have taken that one step further and realize that the craft was my apprenticeship in working with the faeries. I now know that I have emerged from this journey as a *Faerie Priestess*, borrowing many aspects of the craft and melding them together to honour the faeries as a life pathway. Such has been the faeries' impact on my life that we have even given our two children names associated with the faeries. In fact, we do believe that their names were given to us.

In my role as a faerie priestess, I believe that my task is to serve. My initiation with the faeries clarified this for me, for on that magical night when Queen Mab took me from my sleep, she was asking me to take on a vocation for her. In the visitation dream, I helped people to enter Faerie Land and that is what she wishes me to do in real life. This is why I have felt impelled for so long to write this book for you, the faerie seeker.

Today I bring the faeries' vision to people by hosting faeriecraft talks and workshops and using my profession as a writer to bring their message to a mass audience.

One last tale of my fey encounters, an experience that left a profound impression on me... It was Hallowe'en/ Samhain 2000 and I was sitting meditating. The meditation journey that I received was a vivid and all-encompassing experience.

As soon as I closed my eyes, I felt myself to be standing at the foot of Glastonbury Tor, all alone on a very dark night. I was suddenly lifted at great speed up the Tor and deposited inside the tower. A door opened up in the stone floor, only it was not a real door but an astral one, and I could see that it was transparent. As soon as I saw the door open, I seemed to know that it was an invitation for me to enter. I knew that Glastonbury Tor was a gateway to Faerie Land and the Otherworlds. I was not to be disappointed, for as soon as I had entered the door, I was plunged at very great speed down many long wooden ladders. Very quickly my descent ended and I found myself in a green place, where the light was similar to that of dusk. There were apple trees all around me, and I seemed to be at a party that was in full swing.

I was immediately taken by the hand by a small child with slightly green skin. He whisked me into a dance with several other green children. They were the strangest children I had ever seen, but their energy was infectious. They all grinned toothy smiles, giggling continually with the most wonderful sense of fun. At the same time they emanated a gentleness and an inner beauty, and I felt utterly delighted to be with them. They seemed to want me to have as much fun as possible, and everything they did was centred around green apples. They made me a necklace fashioned from dried apple rings and pips and I felt very magical as I put it around my neck. I played apple bobbing with them, and they all giggled so much as they wiped the water from their faces and then plummeted their heads into the barrel of water once again that I thought they would never recover. They would all cheer exuberantly if one came up with an apple between their teeth. They wore green and brown ragged clothes and they had dirty bare feet and grubby hands, but they were as happy as can be. They finally coaxed me to drink cider with them out of little wooden mugs.

All of a sudden, I knew that I had been there long enough and that I should get back. The little green children kissed my cheeks and hugged me before I found myself shooting back up the wooden ladders after my visit to the Apple Isle.

One of the most important aspects of this magical meditation experience was the faerie folk's enthusiasm for me and the fact that they gave me an apple necklace to take away with me. Indeed, the whole encounter was about apples, which are full of magical symbolism. Long after the meditation, I happened to read in a book that the name Avalon means 'the Place of Apples' and that apples themselves are historically regarded as sacred and magical. If sliced across, the apple displays a five-pointed star or pentagram, a sign of faerie protection and spirituality. Avalon, the place of apples, was once seen as the place of death and rebirth. Yet another initiation: to be given a necklace, the symbolic garment of a priestess. The Faerie Priestess.

3

Open for Me the Sparkling Pathway

How to Begin Working with the Faeries

'I knew she was a faerie woman, for her slight body was tapered and as my eyes ran down her legs, where her feet should have been there was a silvery mist... She blinked up at me, her black eyelashes framing her weed-green eyes. In that blink, I knew beyond all reasoning that I was one like her...'

ALICEN GEDDES-WARD,
'THE KISS OF TWO WORLDS'

The Faerie Altar

You can now embark on creating a faerie altar in your home or garden, if you have one. Both would be desirable, if that is possible. The reason for having a faerie altar in your daily environment is so that you have a physical focus of the unseen realms in your home, your own personal window on Faerie Land if you like. It is a faithful reminder of your spiritual pathway. It can also be a constant comfort to be reminded of faeries every day.

You can create your faerie altar in almost any room of your house, as long as you are there regularly to appreciate it. It can be a single shelf in your living room, a designated corner on your dressing-table or an elaborate dresser used solely for the purpose. It can be as small and inconspicuous or as large and ornate as your personal tastes require.

The reason you are beginning your faeriecraft pathway with the creation of a faerie altar is that you need to build a bridge of intent from this world to the Land of Faerie. You begin with your everyday life, with the mundane, for with the fey, everything that you do on a physical level with a faerie purpose has an influence on the otherworldly level, Faerie Land.

The altar needs to be housed in the north of the room. This is for several very sound reasons. North is considered to be the most sacred direction in faeriecraft, and in all pagan faiths it is held to be the home of the gods. It is also home to the Pole Star, sacred to pagans of ancient times. Also, in the northern hemisphere, the north point is the place through which the sun passes at night. For this reason it represents the most profound aspects of our subconscious minds, the place of magic and mystery. If a northern altar is not convenient, the altar can sometimes be positioned in the centre of a room or garden; however when this is the case, the altar can still face north. (If you should live in the southern hemisphere, you may wish to position your altar in the south, as this is the direction of the nocturnal sun in your part of the earth.)

Particularly relevant to faeriecraft is that the north point is the place of *Caer Arianrhod* or *Caer Siddi*, home to the Mistress of the Otherworld Tower, Arianrhod, moon and spinning Faerie Queen or goddess. Also known as the Spiral Castle, it is the power place magicians visit to be initiated and where the creative among us go to receive inspiration through dreams and the subconscious. It is often also the sacred castle where the dead can rest between incarnations.

The possibilities for decorating your altar are endless and very personal to you, and there are numerous themes which can be explored. For example, you may be attracted to the otherworldliness of faeries and may wish to decorate your altar with all things sparkly. You could use Christmas-tree lights, ornaments of faeries, crystals, feathers and beautiful magical tools such as a wand. Be creative, go mad, sprinkle glitter on the altar cloth and hang some faerie wings above the display!

On the other hand, you may be an earthy type, and the faeries may speak to you through moss, driftwood and the secrecy of tree roots. So you could decorate your altar with a small branch, seashells, snail shells, bark and anything that speaks to you of the magic of nature.

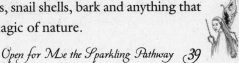

In winter my faerie altar is a simple blend of white and silver, decorated with snowflakes and icicles. I include pictures of Jack Frost and the Snow Queen, both faerie spirits of midwinter. I have little snow faeries hanging from a branch, and silver and white candles to light on the Winter Solstice. I always look forward to putting my winter faerie altar in place, as it reminds me of the magic of winter and my fascination with and love of snow and ice.

A few words of caution on what not to place on your altar: it is inadvisable to have anything that is made from metal, particularly lead, as all faeries have a strong aversion to it. The only permissible metals for use in faeriecraft are gold, silver or copper in their purest forms. Many pagans and witches use athames (ritual knives), which are of course made mostly from metal, and these are often on their altars. A Faerie Priest or Priestess would not use an athame. A wand, preferably homemade, would be a suitable alternative. Tips on wand making and the best materials to use are given further on in the book.

For months just recently the altar in our home was a faerie house constructed by my seven-year-old daughter and her friend. It was made from natural materials and had a frame of wood and large sheets of bark for the roof. The carpet was moss and they had even included a chimney! The faerie house was admired by many visitors who came to our home, as it was beautifully made and took them nearly two days of dedicated hard work to create. In the evenings we lit it with night lights and it looked enchanting and magical, even to the adults who came to see it.

When we wanted to leave an offering, we would leave it on the doorstep!

So you see, the sky's the limit. Your faerie altar can be whatever the faeries mean to you. It can only cease in its creativity where your imagination stops. The faeries deeply appreciate an altar being made in their honour, and this will be a first significant step in reaching out to them. By making an altar, you are also welcoming the faeries into your home and allowing them to see that you wish to form a friendship with them.

A garden altar's appearance and position are more often dictated by the size and design of your plot. The most obvious place to have your altar is of course *at the bottom of the garden*, for there is much truth in the well-known myth that faeries dwell there. The reason for this is that the bottom of the garden is usually the place that is most likely to be forgotten about and maybe a little on the wild side. It is probably the most secret place in the garden. So all in all, it would be the most fitting place to find faeries, taking into account their shyness of humans and their connection with nature.

I have made my garden altars in many varied places, and often they have been overlooked by neighbours' houses. For this reason you sometimes have to be discreet about what you want to include on your altar, as faeries don't like their ways revealed to everyone. A faerie priest or priestess's confidentiality and discretion are much appreciated by the faerie folk, so choose your spot well.

I have had faerie altars on moss-covered tree stumps, under a willow tree, in the middle of a wild flower bed and in the branches of an elder tree. When I have used a tree as my focus, I have always felt inclined to dress the tree as well. This is a wonderfully creative task where you can really use your imagination. I often decorate my trees with little candles placed in the nooks and crannies of the roots and branches. Ribbons also look beautiful and flutter in the breeze. You can use small wind chimes, and I often hang little bells on ribbons from branches too. If the space where I can place offerings is limited, I fill shells, egg cups and thimbles with all the faerie gifts. It is also a chance to really make friends with that tree and the spirit within it. The garden altar should not be too cluttered and needs to blend in well with the rest of nature. You could place crystals, garden ornaments of faeries, flowers, shells, candle lanterns and pots of herbs there.

A faerie altar can also be placed in a wood or other natural setting, such as the banks of a stream or waterfall, or a cave opening or a sacred place. If you choose to have an altar in a natural setting, you must of course be exceptionally respectful of that place and the other people who visit it. An altar in a wild place must always be a temporary altar and must only exist when you are present. Always clear up after yourself, and if you are going to leave something behind, make sure it is very discreet, totally natural and biodegradable.

Our family has adopted the most beautiful tree in our local woods. We call it our *faerie tree,* and whenever we walk in the woods, we always make a beeline for it. The faerie tree has the most intricate and gnarly root structure; in fact the majority of the tree appears to be roots, weaving in and out of one another. Our faerie tree really has to be my favourite altar, as when we go to see it I do feel that we are visiting the faeries. We always take little offerings to the tree, and it is fun for the children to find suitable crevices to place them in.

Faerie Offerings

The main function of an altar, apart from giving you a constant faerie focus, is to provide a place for you to leave faerie offerings. This is an integral part of building a relationship with the fey folk. They want you to communicate with them, tell them your thoughts, express your prayers, spells and wishes. Faeries, as a quirk of their nature, dislike very much being thanked and profuse displays of gratitude. In contrast they do, however, demand respect and appreciate small tokens or gifts, and your physical presence, although it may seem a contradiction, creates a strong impression in Elphame. There is a careful balance to maintain, and you should always be thoughtful in your approach.

Faeries are also very particular about what kind of gift you leave them. First and foremost, make sure it is biodegradable. If possible, try to present it in a natural or biodegradable receptacle too, especially if it is to be left in your garden or a natural setting. Never wrap it in paper or ribbons; remember it is not a person to whom you are giving this gift, but a being of nature. Faeries like the fine but

simple things that the world can offer. Their favourites are
honey, milk, cream, cake, butter and mead. Always make
sure that when you leave a faerie gift it is of the finest that
you can afford and that it is very fresh too.

   If we are visiting our faerie tree in the woods, we fill a
small shell each with honey or milk. We do leave the shells
there, but tucked away from prying eyes. On our next visit

we replace them and take the empty shells home again. Bear in mind that you do not need to leave large amounts (half an empty walnut shell, for instance, will be sufficient), as it is the intention that is important, and the love and emotions that come with the faerie gift that transmit themselves to Faerie Land.

The regularity with which you leave your faerie gifts is a personal thing. It will also depend on the type of altar you have made. If it is an altar within your house, you can leave faerie presents there as regularly as you wish. You may want to do the same in your garden, or only leave presents there at full moons, festivals or when you wish to communicate with the faeries on a particular matter. The faeries will never mind you asking for their help as long as there is an exchange of energy in some way and you are helping them too.

When I am writing, occasionally I feel the need for inspiration. Sometimes it is difficult to focus on the task, or I am just tired. A couple of times during the writing of this book, I have genuinely felt the need for direct faerie contact, reassurance and inspiration. When this has occurred, I have gone into my garden and placed a special bowl full of milk on my garden altar, which is among the flowers at the moment. There I have quietly spoken to Queen Mab of my problem and then gone straight back to my writing desk. On both occasions, as soon as I have put pen to paper I have felt a flood of inspiration and energy and have written more than I usually would. A connection with faeries is a link to the divine and a revealing of the inner self. It is no wonder that I felt my inspiration renewed.

If your altar is in a woodland or another natural setting, you may only take a gift when you get the opportunity to visit. Be ever mindful that the more you visit a wild altar, the stronger your relationship will be with that particular place and the natural energies that dwell there. It does seem easier to sense the presence of faeries in a wild place than in your home or garden and is therefore easier to build a relationship with them there.

The Magical Tides of the Faerie Year

Your altar should be redecorated with the changing of the seasons, as this is a way of connecting with the turning of the year. Your ever-changing altar will allow you to focus on the season and your relationship and emotions surrounding that time of year.

This brings us to the next step on your faeriecraft pathway, one that is a central thread in working with the faeries. The fey people honour the magical tides of the year and they are times of celebration for them. There are eight of these tides, known as festivals or sabbats, which are also observed by wiccans and all pagan pathways. The Summer and Winter Solstices mark the longest and shortest days in the year. The Spring and Autumn Equinoxes then mark the points in the year when night and day are of equal length. You may already be familiar with the names of these festivals, as they are often marked in diaries and calendars, and they are known as *the Lesser Sabbats*. The four remaining sabbats are known as the *fire festivals,* and are called *the Greater Sabbats*. The fire festivals were named after the times when the Celtic peoples of old would light huge bonfires on the hilltops to celebrate these special times. The names for the fire festivals are Imbolc, Beltaine, Lughnasadh ('Loo-nus-uh') and Samhain ('Sow-inn').

These eight festivals mark significant points in the tides of the natural year. Not only do they mark agricultural and sometimes solar tides, but also traditionally magical tides and cycles. Nature affects us on all levels, as anyone who suffers from seasonal affective disorder (SAD) will affirm, and the changing of the seasons also affects psychic, emotional and subconscious tides within us.

The eight sabbats in turn connect us to Faerie Land, as faeries are intrinsic beings of nature and for this reason celebrate the seasonal tides; they are bound to them by the very nature of their existence. These are also times when faeries are most likely to visit us and we may in turn contact them. The most favourable times to see faeries are at any of the eight sabbats or the *between times*. That is when the blurring of the veil between the worlds is most apparent. The between times are dawn, midday, dusk and midnight, all crossover times in our world and therefore magical points in the tides of time. Other likely times are when you are just about to drop off to sleep or when you are just waking, both times when you are neither asleep nor awake. The tides of the moon are also favourable times to commune with the fey folk, a full moon especially, as this is a time of heightened psychic activity and energy.

Some of us will never have the privilege of seeing a faerie either clairvoyantly or in the physical realm. Betty

Ballantine describes this in the foreword to *Faeries* by Brian Froud and Alan Lee: 'Sometimes no amount of mooning around in misty forest glades or communing with nature at the bottom of the garden ... will bring about anything other than a general sense of damp.' So there you have it: following the faeriecraft pathway does not ensure that you will ever be sharing tea at the bottom of your garden with a kindly gnome.

I believe that actually seeing a faerie is a bonus, and the rewards of treading the path of faerie are incredible. The annoying thing for humans is that however much you seek a faerie sighting and visit your faerie altar religiously, the fact of the matter is that you will *always* see a faerie when you are least expecting it. That is the rule. That is the irresistible joke that they have going with humans, and they adore the element of surprise. It may be when you are shelling peas and are musing over what to put in your children's lunchbox the next day.

I heard on a radio programme about a woman who was desperately interested in faeries and had always wanted to see one. One day she was in a great rush to prepare her dinner and go to work (she was a musician and had a concert in the evening). She flung the kitchen bin open to throw in some rubbish and saw a male faerie sitting smiling at her from on top of the potato peelings! It certainly stopped her in her tracks, and her perception of time changed instantly and for some time after that. She seemed to know that the smile meant 'Stop rushing and see the magic in every moment.'

The Eight Sabbats

Here is a guide to the eight sabbats that you can use for changing your altar, focusing on meditation and visualization and celebrating with a faeriecraft ceremony or simply as an excuse to party!

Samhain, 31st October (Greater Sabbat)
Commonly known as Hallowe'en (All Hallows' Eve) and the Celtic new year, this is where the faeries' year begins and that of faeriecraft too. It is the time when the veil between the worlds is at its thinnest and the door to Faerie Land is open for one night.

Midwinter Solstice/Yule, 21st December (Lesser Sabbat) The shortest day and the longest night in the northern hemisphere, this is the time of stillness and rest, focus and reflection. This Solstice marks the crowning of winter and is a day of hope, as this is the last day of the year's darkness. From this day on, the days will slowly lengthen and the light gradually return.

Imbolc, 2nd February (Greater Sabbat) A celebration of the light returning and the days growing longer. The Earth is beginning to stir into growth after its winter rest. This is a time to look ahead, plant ideas and brush away the cobwebs of winter.

Spring Equinox, 21st March (Lesser Sabbat) Day and night are equal length and in the northern hemisphere this is seen as the first day of spring, a time of fertility when the Earth awakens and bursts forth. It is a time to celebrate with the symbolic eggs of new life and to wear a crown of flowers in your hair.

Beltaine, 30th April (Greater Sabbat) Along with Samhain, this is one of the most potent days in the faerie year, when the doorway to Faerie Land is open. It is a time for lovers and weddings and the celebration of the *sacred marriage* of the green goddess and the fecund god which brings forth life in nature. On this pathway, it is also the union of the Faerie King and his Queen. The eve of summer, it is time to dance around the Maypole, wear a crown of hawthorn blossom and truly celebrate the *merry month*.

Midsummer Solstice, 21st June (Lesser Sabbat) This is the longest day of the year in the northern hemisphere and the shortest night. It is the climax of the Earth's cycle of energy and growth, the crowning of summer, but also the last day of summer's fullness, as the light, from this day on, will begin to fade. It is a time of pure celebration, freedom of the self, expression and beauty in all. Wear roses abundantly and unapologetically in your hair!

Lughnasadh, 31st July (Greater Sabbat) This is the ancient feast of the first fruits of the harvest, the time when the Earth's energies first begin to wane and return beneath the land. It is a festival of abundance and fullness, not only of the Earth's fruits, but of the self, an ancient Celtic faerie festival and a time for dance and music.

Autumn Equinox, 21st September (Lesser Sabbat) Day and night are of equal length and in the northern hemisphere this is the day of autumn's end. From this day on, the days will begin to get shorter and the nights will draw in. It is a time of preparation for winter, a time of transition of the Earth's energies, of everything returning to its roots, a time to thank the Earth for summer's abundance, to feast and party. Honour the sacred magical apples of Avalon and drink cider to celebrate.

4

A Goblin Up the Chimney

Faerielore, Cautions and Your Guardian Angel

'...Robin Good-fellow: Are you not he
That frights the maidens of the villagery;
Skims milk, and sometimes labours in the quern,
And bootless makes the breathless housewife churn;
And sometime makes the drink to bear no barm;
Misleads night-wanderers, laughing at their harm?
Those that Hobgoblin call you, and sweet Puck,
You do their work, and they shall have good luck:
Are not you he?'

WILLIAM SHAKESPEARE,
A MIDSUMMER NIGHT'S DREAM

Faerielore and Cautions

Faerielore is a subject in itself, worthy of extensive study. It is steeped in folklore and superstitions and has ancient roots. However, in this book we are not going to concern ourselves with turning our clothes inside out and putting our socks under our beds to protect ourselves from troublesome faerie folk. Practices such as those, quaint and amusing as they are, are best left as folklore. In our vocation as faerie seekers, we require practical advice that can help us to shape our devotional lives in faeriecraft. Commonsense guidelines that can be easily remembered are also important. So what are the most useful facts to keep in mind when working with faerie?

Always, without exception, work with protection. I will describe some protection techniques in further chapters. Laziness and complacency when working with faeries can lead to undesirable results. The ideal situation would be to always work with a friend, so that you can help one another. Since realistically this is not always possible, I cannot stress enough the importance of protection and grounding routines after magical work.

If you visit Faerie Land in a meditation, in a ritual setting, by way of astral travel or even

in a dream, there are strict rules to adhere to.
Never dance or partake of food and drink there,
however tempting it may appear at the time,
for this can lead to faerie entrapment. Witches
are said to be among the only mortals who may
enjoy a certain blurring of the rules. However,
I would never advise putting this theory to the
test, as faerie entrapment is an extremely perilous
occurrence and there are serious penalties to pay
which could alter your life forever.

Do not say thank you to faeries, but leave them a
small gift instead on your faerie altar.

Avoid offending faerie folk, for their feelings are
easily hurt.

Faeries hate iron. If you feel that you are in
genuine danger from malevolent faeries, then
carrying a small piece of iron with you and
sleeping with it under your bed should ensure
your protection. I once had a problematic faerie
and the only iron I had at the time was an iron
saucepan lid. I placed this under my bed and
duly went to sleep. I was awoken in the night
by faerie giggles in my room, as they obviously
thought it was quite hilarious that I should use a

saucepan lid in my defence. I thought I had the last laugh, though, as they never bothered me again!

A Place of Stars

Throughout this book you will notice that I will describe Faerie Land as an *astral* place and the faeries who inhabit that realm as *astral* beings. An understanding of this term is useful as part of the terminology used in faeriecraft. The astral realm is an otherworldly place, and the term *astral* originates from the Latin word *astrum*, meaning 'a star'. The astral realm is not above us in the actual place of stars, but a world that exists as part of the fabric of our own three-dimensional world, a world within a world.

The astral realm has a different quality from that of our physical world. It is a place where linear time does not exist and time as we know it is a stretchy, changeable concept. Energy exists at a higher vibrational frequency, where dreams and thoughts are tangible. Belief in the astral realm is an ancient one, and philosophers throughout history have recognized it and attempted to define it. In the nineteenth century Francis Barrett wrote in *The Magus* how the astral realm was integral to the function of magic. This is because the astral plane is a magical counterpart to our own world where thoughts hold power and are able to manifest, since positive and directed thought are fundamental to the process of magical practice.

Faeries who belong to the astral realm are made of astral light, believed to be a star-like eminence of beauty and purity. We as humans also have our own astral body which exists in harmony with our physical body, unless it breaks free during dreams or an intentional magical act to *astral travel*. With our astral body we may visit Faerie Land and are linked to our physical selves by a cord of light, according to pagan beliefs. Once we die, our astral body leaves the physical body and the astral cord is broken. Visiting the astral realms can be a blissful experience, and you may even have done it already, without realizing it, in your dreams. However, intentional, conscious astral travel should never be attempted without the proper instruction of an experienced Faerie Priest or Priestess.

The Astral Bender

This is my own term, brought about by my familiarity with the state, although I am not alone in experiencing this condition. Needless to say, I am now very vigilant about avoiding this common state, and I would like to persuade you to avoid it too. I will explain.

Faerie Land, although beautiful and alluringly magical, is also a dangerous place for humans. It is quite acceptable for us to visit temporarily and vice versa for faeries to visit our dimension. However, the astral bender comes about when we don't quite come back and the danger of the situation is that people don't usually realize it. Here are the symptoms of someone on a classic astral bender:

You are in a strange state of constant arousal. You feel excited about something, but are not quite sure what it is.

Your body also reacts as if it is excited or aroused. You sweat more, you feel nervous tension and you are restless for no apparent reason. You may also feel sexually aroused and be unable to switch this feeling off.

You feel what a friend once described to me as *headish*. This means that you are constantly existing in your imagination and feel unable to concentrate properly on normal everyday tasks. In fact, you may not even care very much about mundane matters. You may drive a little more recklessly or forget to switch the gas burner off, for example.

An astral bender is strangely pleasurable and comfortable. There can be no desire to become grounded, as the feeling excites your senses and your imagination. You may experience a heightened sense of imagination, and this is all the more alluring. However, when on an astral bender your physical body and your astral body are not aligned or in balance, as you are existing partly on the astral plane. Prolonged exposure to the state can lead to depression and health problems.

The most difficult aspect of this condition is recognizing that it is actually happening to you. I called it a *bender* because it can be very pleasurable for a while, although after a time it will become a half-existence that can sometimes make you feel as if you are going mad. It is also a very lonely feeling, as the symptoms are very hard to pin down, and of course you will not find them in any medical book. You will just know that you are feeling very weird and definitely not right.

Faerie Land will draw you in, have no doubt about that. The world of faerie is full of magical power, enchantments, alluring beauty and intricate emotions. It is very easy for it to be romanticized and the dangers glossed over with sparkles and glitter and images of harmless flower faeries. Faerie Land is a magic mirror, a place of peace, but it is also a place of danger and terror if you let it be.

If you recognize that you are on an astral bender, take action immediately. Talking to someone who will understand your situation can bring you back down to earth. Releasing emotions can also help, as can focusing on your physical body. Coming back is mainly up to you, and you need to be strong about your desire to exist fully in the physical realms.

To avoid astral benders, those who follow faeriecraft must be particularly careful about protection and grounding. I will deal with grounding techniques more thoroughly in Chapter 7. This is when we will begin to work on a more psychic level with faerie.

Those Little Hobgoblin Problems

As with people, unfortunately not all faeries are ones whose company you would like to share. If you are always working with benevolent intentions, asking for protection in all your magical work and generally following the faeriecraft pathway with a sensible and responsible attitude, malevolent or mischievous faeries should be a problem you only encounter rarely, perhaps once or twice in a lifetime. Indeed, there is very little to worry about if you do come across them, as they are often more annoying than dangerous. However, faeries own the 'T' in tricky and once you have an unpleasant faerie in your vicinity, then you'll soon want to be rid of it.

I have had many encounters with troublesome faeries, but this is only because word seems to have got around that I know how to sort them out. So I do get the odd phone call when I am asked if I can go along and banish a faerie from a house. These beings are most often seen by children and lurk about in their bedrooms, invading their sleep and colouring their dreams with nightmares. This usually goes hand in hand with other disturbances in the house, such as icy patches in certain rooms and things that the adults notice too, such as marked runs of bad luck, objects going missing around the house and turning up in odd places. There may be also be a feeling of a general cloud of discord hanging over the house and its occupants.

Once when working a ritual with my group, at the beginning of the rite we all felt a gust of icy wind blow down the chimney and swirl around our ankles. So dramatic was the event that someone joked that we had an uninvited guest amongst us in our circle. That made us all laugh, and then we thought no more of it for a while. That is, until odd things began to happen later on during our group meditation. Some of us had an uneasy feeling and we could not explain why we did it, but another member and I felt impelled to open our eyes. We both saw the same thing: a three-foot goblin standing by our altar, watching us all in meditation. We knew he was up to no good. Everyone was immediately alerted, the goblin banished and the ritual closed. The next day the house was cleansed and blessed.

Goblin, Begone!

If you find yourself in the company of a mischievous fey, here's how to deal with it successfully.

Incidentally, most faeries in this category are lumped under the generic term *goblin* or *hobgoblin*, if you have the need to address them. One thing when addressing a goblin or similar is never to be polite. If you ask a goblin to leave politely, they will simply laugh at you.

Also, do not suffer their company for any longer than you need to. I was once asked by someone who had a goblin in their house, 'Should I ask them why they are here and what they want with me?' *'Absolutely not'* was and always will be my answer. You must not let them have any chance of conversation, as they will make mischief at any opportunity. Their sole purpose is mischief, and that is all you need to know.

You also need to be armed with the fact that the goblin should be scared of you and not the other way around.

Your attitude should be one of outrage. How dare they come into your house and cause a disturbance! You are the Faerie Priest or Priestess and you work with good energies, a much more powerful force than the low-life meddling world that they belong to. Confidence is important, since if you're shaking like a leaf and throwing salt water at arm's length, you probably won't look a very forbidding sight. That goblin needs to be shaking in their boots, and if that means that you have to invite a sympathetic friend along for moral support, then so be it!

There are a few things you will need to perform a goblin banishment:

ordinary cinnamon from your kitchen cupboard
charcoal
an incense burner
salt and water

To begin with, ask your guardian angel for help. You can even visualize them wrapping their beautiful wings around you. Then light your charcoal and as this is igniting, consecrate your salt and water (see pages 228–29) and then mix them together in a bowl.

Once your charcoal has turned grey, sprinkle about half a teaspoon of cinnamon on it, which will produce a lot of smoke. Imagine that the smoke is driving out the goblin. See them coughing and spluttering on your smoke. Actually open a window or door to let the smoke out and with it the goblin.

Once you have visualized the offending being leaving, demand that it leaves and give no room for doubt in what you mean. When addressing faeries, they prefer rhyme, especially if this is some sort of instruction. Your words should be your own, but can go something like this:

> 'Goblin with your ugly face,
> Leave here now with good grace.
> Don't bother coming back at all,
> or a nasty fate will you befall.
> I banish you in the name of
> the Faerie Queen!'

Don't hesitate to insult, threaten and most importantly swear at the goblin. Swearing is the thing they dislike the most and it usually does the trick. Now this may not sound like the behaviour of one on a spiritual pathway. However, it is the only effective method of banishing goblins and you have to show them that you mean business.

Then, working clockwise around the room, sprinkle your salt water and continue to demand that they leave, otherwise they will have the wrath of the Faerie Queen to deal with. *The angrier and scarier you appear, the quicker they will depart. Most importantly, be confident in the belief that they will be banished.*

Once you have seen or felt the goblin withdraw, you will know this moment as the atmosphere in the room immediately lifts, as if the whole room has been filled with fresh air.

After they have gone, you need to open the windows for a couple of hours. This is because their presence can leave a residue, characterized by an unpleasant feeling. However this should lift very quickly and will have disappeared within 24 hours at most.

Continue to burn cinnamon for a while and visualize the room being filled with love. Playing beautiful music can help, as can anything that replaces the negative atmosphere with an ambient positive one.

Thank your guardian angel and leave a present on your faerie altar for the Faerie Queen.

You may never need the information in this chapter, and I hope that you never have a goblin in your chimney! Although if you do find yourself in a slightly sticky situation or you know someone else who needs help, you will know exactly what to do. When I had a conversation with my mum one day about getting rid of a goblin someone was having trouble with in their house, she said, 'It sounds like you live in a Harry Potter book'. It sounds a bit ridiculous to me too sometimes, but I know that I have felt incredibly empowered by being able to help people in this way.

A goblin will always teach you something too. They may be an unwelcome faerie, but all fey encounters uncover something in the deeper you, something that you may not have wanted to face. Sometimes it takes a goblin to unearth it.

The Angel Cousins

Angels and faeries are so closely linked that to work with one or the other exclusively is virtually impossible. A crossover is always likely and in fact desirable. Angels and faeries complement one another in their roles and their relationship with humanity and the Earth. No book on faeriecraft could be complete without including some insight into the realm of the angels and their work.

You will be able to work with your guardian angel alongside the faeries, melding the two celestial cousins together to complete a happy marriage. Your guardian angel, whether you have encountered them yet or not, is the overseer of the faeriecraft pathway. In this chapter we will be exploring how to unite your guardian angel with faeriecraft by visualization and exercises

on how to contact your angel and how to work with them harmoniously for protection and guidance.

There is a widely held misconception that angels are uniquely Christian deities. However, this is untrue, as angels are recognized by most faiths and, like the faeries, they are for everyone and serve humanity as a whole. Faeries are the embodiment of the earth's consciousness, and angels are the manifestation of the universe and a link to our creator. The word *angel* is derived from the Greek *angelos*, which means 'messenger'. Throughout history angels have been thought to be messengers from God. They are our link to the divine, helping us in our soul's journey and gently highlighting wisdom, beauty, benevolence and trust in our world.

Angelic beings have been with us since long before the rise of Christianity; and our ancestors have passed down paintings, stories and images to show the validity of these beings. However, with the coming of the New Age, the time that we are living through now, angels and faeries are drawing nearer to us to guide us through this transitional period. As a result of this, we are experiencing an angel renaissance. Angels have been influencing artistic people through paintings, poetry and songs, photography, sculpture and all art forms. There has been an explosion of interest in all things angelic in many areas of spirituality. This angelic resurgence in our culture proves that as a race we have acknowledged the subtle presence of the angels drawing closer to us.

Like faeries, angels have natures which are very different from humans'. Angelic beings vibrate at a much faster and higher level than us and, also like faeries, are perceived in many different ways. Angels are also neither male nor female but androgynous having the qualities of both sexes. It is possible to perceive an angel as belonging to either one sex or the other. However, this is because they have chosen to show themselves to you in this manner.

To have complete knowledge of the faeries, the faerie seeker must also have experience of the angelic realms. Here we will explore these realms in more depth.

Your Guardian Angel

There are many realms that the angels inhabit. These range from the worlds of the angels and the archangels right through to those of the cherubim and seraphim at the very top of the spheres of heavenly beings. At this place and time, the angelic being that you need to focus on is your guardian angel. Everyone has a guardian angel aligned to their soul and their life's pathway. Of all the spheres of heavenly beings, the guardian angels are the ones who are closest to humanity.

If you have chosen faeriecraft as your spiritual pathway, then your guardian angel will already be expecting you to contact them. They are there for you as an independent guide, to oversee your pathway and help you if you ask for assistance.

I have personally always included angels in my faeriecraft. The faeries are really at the forefront of my daily life. However, I always know that I can call upon my guardian angel if I need to, and it feels as though the angels are there as another link to the divine. Faeries are of course a link to the divine as well, but to a different facet. If you include your guardian angel in your faeriecraft, then you will find that your spiritual life will be more rounded, as the faeries and angels do complement one another. Together in one craft, they complete a balanced pathway.

I would like to share with you an experience I had with my guardian angel. It was the year 2000 and at the time I was heavily pregnant with my son. The encounter happened at night and Neil was working away, so on that occasion I was alone, except for my then four-year-old daughter. I had had an ordinary dream, which now I cannot recollect, but during this uneventful dream I seemed to be pulled awake while still sleeping, a contradiction it would seem, but that is exactly what it felt like. I knew that I was inhabiting a new place and state entirely, and I have since also learned that what I experienced was called a *visitation dream*.

I suddenly found myself sitting on the edge of an office desk, but there were no surroundings, no room, no place but the desk. A blond man of about my age stood before me and I instantly recognized him. However, I knew that I had never met him before, not in my physical life anyway. He seemed to know me and greeted me as if I were an old and loved lifelong friend. I accepted this and trusted him at once. He wore a grey business suit and he spoke no words to me. He simply smiled warmly and then enfolded me within his arms in an embrace. As I was within his arms, I felt peculiarly and overwhelmingly as if he was comforting me for my life, as if I needed him and he had been sent by someone. The energy of love which he brought with him was evident on first meeting him, and I felt encircled by an incredibly beautiful sense of God's love or divine love. The feeling that he had been *sent* to me was all-encompassing.

The embrace ended and we parted and then he was gone. As I awoke, I expected to be alone, but instead felt what I thought to be the hand of an angel stroking my fingers ever so gently and beautifully. For a few moments I was in a blissful state, not quite awake yet and still bathed in the presence of angels. When I awoke properly, I discovered that it was my daughter, who was stroking my fingers in her sleep. Unbeknown to me, she had climbed into my bed in the early hours of the morning while I was still asleep. In those moments, all life contained goodness.

As I drove my daughter to kindergarten that same morning, I could think of nothing but the visitation dream. Strangely, everything seemed to hold a magical quality: the fields glistened with sparkling dew and looked alive to me, people seemed to smile more and the children at school appeared unusually peaceful.

At the time I did not recognize the man as my guardian angel. He did not have huge feathered wings for a start! But shortly after the visitation, I felt I had some sort of answer as to why I should have an intense spiritual experience at that time in my life. It was planned that I would have a home birth and I went in for a last scan, the only reason being that I was changing consultants and the new doctor wanted to check that everything was okay. It was not. I was diagnosed with major placenta praevia very late in pregnancy. The consultant could not understand why this had not been diagnosed previously, as there are obvious and dramatic symptoms with this condition, but I displayed none of them. If I had not had the scan, I would have gone ahead with a home birth. With this condition, if I had gone into natural labour at home I would probably have bled to death and my son would have suffocated before he was born. So, without knowing it, both my son and I were in great danger at the time of the visitation.

My son was subsequently born by Caesarean section three weeks early, and the consultant commented during the operation that my birth canal was indeed completely blocked and that natural birth would have been impossible and fatal. This was a very traumatic time.

Five months later I was still puzzling about the visitation and wrote the encounter down. I wondered why it had happened and why it had had such a profound effect. I began to fit everything together in my mind. I had the conviction that the man had been sent, and I also felt as if I had been in the presence of God and, after the dream, angels. Then the realization that my guardian angel had paid me a visit came to me. It seemed so obvious in hindsight, but it took me a long while to work it out!

There still seemed to be holes in the visitation: why hadn't he appeared to me as a traditional angel for one thing? Why had we been near an office desk, and why had he been dressed in a suit? It took me a further couple of years to work all that out! It wasn't as if I was constantly on the guardian angel case, you understand, but every so often my mind would go back to the visitation and it would seriously bug me that I hadn't gotten all the answers. Of course all these things come to us in coded messages. The fact that I was sitting on the desk meant to me that it was my work desk and the angel was coming to visit me there. He came in a suit, in a businesslike capacity, and I took this to mean that my guardian angel will visit me in my work (faeriecraft and writing) and will help me in an angelic capacity. We had formed a working partnership, and his visit was partly to tell me this.

I have always been eternally grateful for that angel visitation. It gave me such comfort at that time in my life, and the experience was so strong and so incredibly powerful that I only have to remember it to feel comforted in tough times.

Such is the power of the angels.

Contacting your Guardian Angel

Angels work on the 'seek and you shall find' assumption. In other words, they rarely speak unless they are spoken to, and they need you to make contact with them in order for a connection to begin to flow. Your guardian actively requires you to ask to be able to converse with you. So just because you have not heard or seen your angel before does not mean that you do not have one. Of course we do hear occasionally of people who have angelic experiences quite spontaneously, with no prior contact on their part. Like the faeries, the angels also have a wondrously unpredictable nature and, like all divine beings, they often work in *mysterious ways*. The golden rule for working consciously and purposefully with your angel is to contact them and seek a relationship, and here's how.

There are many ways to contact your guardian angel, and one of the most effective is through meditation. Meditation allows you to listen and experience the other realms. It is focused listening. However, before you leap into angel meditations, there are some things you can do to get ready.

Many of the rules that apply to faerie contact also apply to angels. You may remember that everything you do in your physical life makes a great impact on the Otherworlds, so with this in mind, here's how you can start.

Writing your guardian angel a letter is a magical act and can be your starting-point. This can be on paper or on your computer, but remember that this is a magical letter and not just some note to the milkman! Choose some really special paper or parchment. Make it coloured paper if you feel drawn to a particular colour, and use a fountain pen, coloured pencils or coloured ink. Any magic, on whatever level, works on the principle that the more effort and thought you put into it, the better the results you will achieve. This is because magic is a concentration of the mind to gain an outcome desirous to your will. The more you focus on a magical act, the more successful you will be. So if you are writing your angel letter on the computer, seek out a beautiful font and some background illustrations, for example. Make your letter a thing of beauty.

Your guardian angel has been with you all your life, so there is no need to make your letter formal or serious. Angels, like faeries, have a sense of fun and freedom and connect well with the realm of the imagination. They exist on the love vibration, so above all this letter should come from the heart. It is also important to get straight to the point, as angels require a clear message from you for the communication to work. In your first letter, tell your angel how much you would like to get to know them and work with them. Let them know when and where you intend to begin your angel meditation and convey your feelings about this. Angels connect with your emotions, so you can include anything important about this time in your life. Remember to be clear and concise and you will have worked your magic well.

Once you have written your letter, you can decorate it in any way that reminds you of angels: glitter, stars, sequins or small white feathers. As with your faerie altar, it is your imagination that is the most important concept here. So really go to town – choose a gold envelope, for example, or write your letter with a silver pen. The choice is yours!

When you have finished, put your letter somewhere really special. This could be on your faerie altar, in a secret drawer, under a crystal, next to some beautiful flowers or inside the pages of a book that is meaningful to you. Wherever you place your angel letter, make sure that it means something to you, for the emotions that led you to that place will send the letter to the angel.

If you find writing letters difficult, there are other equally imaginative ways in which to initiate contact with your guardian angel. If you enjoy art, then paint or draw them a picture. Again choose special paper, address the picture to your angel and convey your feelings to them through the colours and forms that you create on the paper or canvas. When you have finished your picture, you may like to fold it up like a letter and put it in a special place, or you could consider framing it and hanging it above your faerie altar.

If you are neither drawn to letters nor images, then maybe you would prefer to send a message to your angel straight through the ether. This is also a lovely thing to do if you have children, because they can join in too. You should ideally choose a beautiful place outside. Your garden will do if you have one, or you could be beside a running stream, in a meadow or even up a tree! If you do not have access to open spaces, then a city park or balcony would be fine. As long as you are in touch with the element of air, then this will work.

All you need is a child's bottle of bubble mixture, the type that comes with a bubble wand. Sit down and concentrate on what you would like to say to your angel, remembering to be clear and to speak from the heart.

Now imagine that each bubble is a message that you are sending to your guardian angel. As each stream of bubbles is blown out into the air, imagine that your message is held inside the bubbles. Remember, thoughts are things, and as long as you put them in a physical vessel of some kind, they

will reach their destination intact, just as if you were to send thoughts to your best friend they might not be able to pick them up, but if you were to put your message in a letter and send it, they would receive it. Even though astral postmen don't exist as such, the elements can act as thought carriers. A bubble on the breeze, a letter on the fire spiralling in smoke, a bottle on the water with a message inside, a letter buried in the earth or placed under a stone, these are all elemental message carriers and ways of contacting your angel through the magic of the natural world. Always flow with nature and its tides and elements if you can.

Begin to get into the habit of talking to your guardian angel. You can ask them to contact you through your dreams. Angels are *messengers,* and the dream state is an easier way for them to make contact with you and bring messages, as you are more receptive while sleeping. Keeping a dream diary by your bed is a good idea so that you can record any nocturnal angel messages. Dreams are often extremely vivid at the time, but they quickly become blurred and faded. For this reason, it's helpful to write your angel dreams down.

Another good reason for recording dreams on paper is that the coded messages sent by angels are not always clear at the time of receiving them. By reading them back, you can see more clearly and objectively what their true meaning may be.

As with your angel letter, make your dream diary a sacred object, and put as much of your own energy into it as possible. It need only be a plain notebook which you can buy from any newsagent's, but make it magical. Cover it with handmade paper, for example, and add ribbons as page markers. Write in it with a special pen or coloured ink, and illustrate your dream diary with drawings. If you are not on the artistic side, then cut out pictures from magazines or stick in silver stars. Be creative and dedicate your dream diary to the angels. Keep it by the side of your bed at all times, and expect magical dreams when you are least expecting them!

Once you have contacted your guardian angel in your physical life, then it's time to cross the astral bridge to the realm of visualization. Add something special to your faerie altar in dedication of your angel. It may be something as simple as a white feather or a picture of an angel or an object that symbolizes events in an angel dream. The choice is a personal one between you and your angel.

The Angel Wings Visualization

Your angel is the ultimate overseer of the faeriecraft pathway and the celestial guardian of your spiritual life. They are dependable, loving, wise and have your interests as their top priority. Here I will gently guide you to meet your guardian angel.

When working with angels, I burn a candle in one of the celestial colours of white, silver or gold. You might like to do the same. Prepare yourself by relaxing in a sitting position. Close your eyes and breathe deeply. Ask your guardian angel for protection. You are now ready to be enfolded within the wings of your angel.

~~~~~~~

See yourself being surrounded by sparkling white light, a light that could only be celestial in origin. The light fills your aura, shimmering and twinkling, as if it contains a million tiny stars. As you become bathed in the luminescent glow, it emanates a feeling of peace. Allow yourself to feel at peace and rest in the radiance of its beautiful energy. Know that you are safe and being held by the goodness of the universe. Relax into a peaceful state for a few moments and concentrate on the enveloping light.

After a while the white light begins to become energized and almost pulsates. Behind you, you *sense* a loving presence *arriving*. Very slowly you feel two enormous feathered wings reach around your body, as if they are screening and protecting you from any negativity. Allow the wings to enfold you and softly bring a feeling of pure love and devotion. You are in the arms of your guardian angel.

You may wish to see more of your angel at this stage or you may not. If you would like to, you may visualize yourself looking up to see them above you. They may show themselves to you in this visualization or they may leave this for another time. Just accept what happens and know that they are working with your best interests at heart. You may stay within the wings of your angel for as long as you like.

When you feel that it is a comfortable time to move on, you can visualize your faeriecraft pathway. See a footpath in the countryside before you. You may be walking through a meadow of wild flowers and sweet grasses or a woodland pathway covered in scrunchy leaves and flanked by trees. The type of pathway is your choice, but it does symbolize your spiritual pathway with the faeries, so make it a beautiful image, perhaps filled with butterflies and crystals, running streams and spiders' webs glistening with dew. Make it a pathway that you would definitely delight in treading.

Now visualize yourself walking along that footpath, and see your guardian angel walking by your side. Visualize this image strongly. See yourself and your guardian angel surrounded by the lovely luminescent white light. Stand back and see yourself and your angel both walking along the pathway until you have disappeared over the horizon. By going through this process, you are symbolically calling upon the assistance and protection of your guardian angel.

Now free your mind of the pathway visualization and come back to yourself, with your angel ever present behind you. Thank your angel, either mentally or verbally, and send out loving thoughts to them. Feel the angel's wings gently releasing you from their enfoldment and as they do so the glow of the celestial white light begins to fade. After a few moments, you see yourself as you were before you began to visualize.

When you are ready, you may open your eyes and eat and drink. You can also leave a little thank you token on your faerie altar to acknowledge your experience with your angel.

You might like to record your results from this and other visualizations by writing them down afterwards so that you don't miss any vital messages.

Keeping Your Angel Wings

Now that you have become acquainted with your guardian angel and have worked with them in visualization, you can weave angels in and out of your faerie pathway in whatever way you choose, whenever the need arises. You can incorporate working with your angel into your own rituals, pathworkings, spells, wishcraft, protection, faerie altar and every aspect of your spiritual pathway and mundane life too.

Don't forget to talk to your angel often. You can sometimes communicate by writing a letter or painting a picture, for example. Keep the communication channels fluid and contact your angel often, not just when you are in need of help.

5

The Kiss of the Faerie Queen

The Faerie Queens and How to Work with Them

'I am but the queen of fair Elfland,
And I'm come here foe to visit thee.
...she turned about her milk-white steed,
And took True Thomas up behind,
And aye wheneer her bridle rang
The steed flew swifter in the wind.'

FRANCIS JAMES CHILD, 'THOMAS THE RHYMER',
THE ENGLISH AND SCOTTISH POPULAR BALLADS

Who Are the Faerie Queens?

In order to work successfully with the faeries, it is essential to form an alliance with one or more of the Faerie Queens. By doing so, you will ensure that you are always working with the highest possible energy in Faerie Land.

Through my research, there seems to be a common thread to the origin of the Faerie Queens. Many of them seem to be intrinsically linked to goddesses. Anna Franklin in *The Illustrated Encyclopaedia of Fairies* tells us of the goddess Holda being 'originally a goddess of the hearth and spinning, demoted to a fairy … in Christian times'. Many goddesses are described not only as faerie goddesses but also as Queens of the Faeries. Diana is another of these. She is primarily cited as a Roman moon goddess in *The Witches' Goddess* by Janet and Stewart Farrar. However, Doreen Valiente in *An ABC of Witchcraft Past and Present* finds that 'the goddess Diana was regarded as Queen of Faerie' by King James I, who wrote *Daemonologie*. This was at a time when the old pagan gods were being demoted to the realms of faerie and sent underground by the wave of Christianity.

There are so many faerie goddesses who are considered to be Queens that it would be impossible to list all of them. Some of them are renowned in history and even literature, while others are so little known that a name is the only information we have about them. Often Faerie Queens are difficult to classify correctly, as there is so much conflicting information. Frequently names are categorized with faerie traits and privileges and subsequently regarded as Faerie Queens, but in some cases they are not. In my opinion this is a matter of interpretation. Also, not all the Queens have clear-cut roles. Many have had lives as mortal women, often linked to royalty, and have become goddesses and also Faerie Queens upon their death. Some roles blur and merge, depending on which book you read. There is little written collectively on Faerie Queens, which is truly astonishing considering the significance they possess when working with the realms of faerie.

Their stories tell enchanted tales of lives woven with magic and legend, of troubles overcome by bravery and womanly guile. Chosen to be Faerie Queens for their intellect, formidability and intoxicating unrivalled beauty, these are enchantresses in a league of their own. Only a fool would challenge a Faerie Queen and expect to win. They demand the deepest respect and command all the magic in Faerie Land.

Working with a Faerie Queen often happens quite naturally, as a particular Faerie Queen may be drawn to you. This can also work the other way around, and it is possible to request a working relationship with a Faerie Queen with whom you feel an affinity. Working with the Faerie Queens offers you unrivalled protection, and they can act as your spiritual guide and guardian. If you should have any problems with their subjects, you can go for them for assistance and advice.

In this chapter we will focus on three of the Queens of Elfland to initiate your connection and illustrate how to call upon them and eventually establish a working affinity.

It's a Guy Thing

I have sometimes been asked whether it's okay for men to contact Faerie Queens and work with them. The answer is that it is completely natural for men to seek contact with a Faerie Queen and form a working relationship, and this goes for women working with Faerie Kings too. Many male pagans and wiccans work with goddesses and the female energy, and this translates to faeriecraft and its fey Queens.

Men who are attracted to faeriecraft as a spiritual pathway are more likely than the average man to be in touch with their feminine side, or anima, as it is known. In women, the masculine elements are known as the animus. For a man to be influenced by his anima is a totally positive attribute and does not in any way mean he is effeminate. The feminine energy within us all is responsible, among other things, for creativity, sensitivity, nurturing, caring and magic. These wonderful qualities can equally be conveyed by a male personality, and how enlightening and beautiful it can be when this is so.

For a man, working with a Faerie Queen will unearth his anima and help him to develop that most feminine of all energies, magic. Once the anima has been lifted from its shadow, a man following faeriecraft should be able to fully embrace the divine within himself.

Faerie Queens can seem, especially to men, to be sexually alluring, beautiful, bewitching and powerful creatures. For some men the decision to work with a particular Faerie Queen may be partly a sexual pull. This is common and perfectly okay. All faeries belong to nature, which is continually reproducing in all its forms, and faeries reflect the natural world. You could almost say that they are fecundity personified. A Faerie Queen is of course the most potent possessor of that natural force. Sexual energy is also an extremely powerful magical tool, and learning to channel this form of universal vitality is all part of the magical training bestowed by the faerie monarchy. However, this is only one facet of their many qualities on a well-balanced pathway and should not be the *only* aspect which draws you to a particular Faerie Queen.

How to Work with a Faerie Queen

The desire to work with a Faerie Queen is among the most important aspects of beginning your work. You may not already have a particular Queen in mind or be especially drawn to any one of them. I do not believe that this matters. As long as you have the desire to make a connection, the faeries will have a plan for you.

Both the Faerie Queens that I work with predominantly made themselves known to me and not the other way around. My story illustrates how desire alone can produce results.

Winter is one of my favourite seasons. I am intrigued by snow and snowflakes. When it snows I have always had a sense of excitement and felt particularly empowered. This feeling increased through my teens and as the craft found me. One evening after it had snowed heavily, I felt an impulse to go into my garden. I stood alone in the darkness, seeing the glinting, sparkling magical blanket of snow beneath my feet. The snow made me feel incredibly charged, magical and powerful, but I had no idea why. I raised my arms above my head and stretched them towards the sky. I did not know then that this was the goddess position, I just moved into it instinctively. I wanted to say thank you for the snow and my exuberance because of it. However, knowing nothing of goddesses or Faerie Queens at that time, the only deity I knew to thank was my childhood favourite, the Snow Queen. I felt a little silly on my own in the garden, saying thank you to a fairytale character. It was akin to expressing my thanks to Cinderella or Sleeping Beauty. In a peculiar way, though, it felt completely natural, and I felt a very real connection on many levels with the Snow Queen that night. On leaving the snowy garden, feeling more alive and invigorated than I had ever done before, I knew my desire was to encounter that feeling once again.

The experience was on my mind for the next few weeks, and the vivid event left an impression on me. The following summer, Neil and I attended a guided walk in London's Greenwich Park. Unbeknown to me at the time, this is thought to be the Snow Queen's spiritual home in Britain. Imagine my excitement when our guide, the author Jack Gale, stopped at a dip in the earth and explained that this was known as the Snow Well. The only recorded evidence for this is a bill for repair, dated 1637 and issued by the Queen's House, which is situated in the grounds of the park, referring to it as 'the Snow Well'. However, the site is referred to as such and its existence is reinforced by the proximity of local names completing the wintry picture of perhaps the Snow Queen's influence on Greenwich. Locally there are Snow Hill, Plum Pudding Hill and the White House, all fitting into a convincing argument for the historic presence of a snow-bearing figure. To the south of the Snow Well are Germanic burial mounds, a possible indication of an essentially Germanic goddess being worshipped in Greenwich. As well as all these tangible pointers, there is a plethora of anecdotal evidence of people experiencing the Snow Queen there, which has been documented by Jack Gale in his book *Goddesses, Guardians and Groves*.

I saw the Snow Queen standing in the well. There were whirling snow flurries all around her. Her gaze was fixed upon me all the while. I barely heard Jack explaining the history of the Snow Well, though he seemed to be saying that the Snow Queen was not just a Hans Christian Andersen fairy tale, but a goddess. The fairy tale came much later and portrayed her as a wicked queen, cruel to children and extremely vain. Nothing could be further from the truth, as the real goddess, named Holda, among other derivative names, was of Germanic origin and known to love animals and children and generally be of a benevolent nature. So it was, on a hot summer's day in Greenwich Park, that the Snow Queen made herself known to me, and things were never quite the same again.

From that day on, I began to research more into the goddess of snow and winter. In the December of 1996 Neil designed a Yule card to send to our family and friends. It depicted the Snow Queen flying over the snowy rooftops of a town at night, snow falling from her fingertips onto the town below. The very next day I delivered this card to a friend, and we were standing chatting at her fireplace while she opened the envelope. As she took the card out, she looked up at me speechless, a look of complete shock on her face. She looked so astounded, I wondered what on earth the matter could be. After a moment she regained her composure and explained breathlessly that the picture on the card was exactly the dream she had had the night before, only instead of the Snow Queen, it had been me in her dream, flying over her house with snow falling from my hands onto her roof. She was completely unaware of my interest in the Snow Queen at the time, as I had only ever discussed it with Neil.

Since then there have been numerous instances of friends seeing me appear to them as the Snow Queen. This has happened in dreams and meditation and as transfiguration. All these experiences have made me feel spiritually attuned to her. I now consider her to be one of my faerie guides. In meditations and dreams she has always appeared to me with a procession of faeries behind her. It was not until quite recently that I read in several sources that she was a faerie goddess and also a Faerie Queen. That confirmed to me all the more that I am meant to work with her.

To work with a Faerie Queen, you simply need to acknowledge the desire. Think about a Faerie Queen in your imagination, daydream about her, doodle sketches of her and write her poetry. Leave offerings for her on your faerie altar and definitely get used to magical happenings! No two people will have the same experiences, and she will *always* make herself known to you when you are least expecting it.

If you have a particular Queen in mind, then meditation is an excellent way of reaching out to her. I believe that it is counterproductive to dwell on the details of faerie history, for information is hugely contradictory from source to source and open to interpretation. Also, as soon as you begin to get bogged down with historical details, you very quickly lose the magic and inspiration. What is important is the spirit in which Faerie Queens come to us and on what spiritual level we can work with them. That is why, as well as giving a brief history of each of the three Queens below, I have given a psychic impression of them.

Now we will explore three of the Faerie Queens and how to work with them.

The Snow Queen

Unlike the other Faerie Queens that I have highlighted in this chapter, the Snow Queen does not have mortal origins. Her origins are truly celestial. She is also known as Frau Hölle, Holda and Dame Venus, and appears to be interchangeable as a goddess and Faerie Queen figure. She is reputed to be the daughter of the Aesir god Loki and is associated with many cultures throughout the northern hemisphere, although she is particularly identified with Germany, Denmark and (a little-known fact) Britain, according to the author Jack Gale. Her story is that she is a stunningly beautiful witch of Teutonic folklore. At the Winter Solstice she rides through the snow-laden skies, shaking her pillows

as she flies on her chariot and making the snow fall. She is known as a sky goddess, and the company she keeps is called the Wild Hunt. They soar through the winter skies bringing snowstorms until Twelfth Night.

The Snow Queen is also known to transform from a heavenly enchantress into a hag faerie, known as Frau Hölle or Mother Goose, who rides the snowy skies on a swan or goose. Christianity demoted and demonized her into a wicked child-stealing seductress, and this was reinforced by her portrayal in *The Lion, the Witch and the Wardrobe* by C. S. Lewis and in Hans Christian Andersen's fairy tale. However, the snow faerie is making a divine comeback, determined to mend her distorted image and take her rightful place on her icicled throne.

Originally she was a goddess associated with spinning, the hearth and housework. She is identified with holy wells, water and lakes, and her underground ice palace is accessed via a well. Here she presides over the wintry season. Her companions are wolves, horses, bears, geese, dogs, cats and hawks, all considered to be her sacred animals. As I discovered, one of her sacred sites in Britain is acknowledged to be the Snow Well in Greenwich Park. As with many of the Faerie Queens, she exudes a potent sexual energy and is beguilingly beautiful and bewitching.

Tuning into the Snow Queen's dynamic persona and energies, I received these images:

The Snow Queen's Impression

The Snow Queen showed herself to me in a resplendent white sparkling dress. She was bathed in the most beautiful white light, and I felt her presence to be immense. She was at the head of a procession through a snowy landscape in the dead of night. I could see moonlight shining on the deep snow, making it sparkle and appear quite magical. It was a sharp, cold, clear night and the stars shone crystalline and strong in the black night's sky. Behind the Snow Queen in the procession were lantern-bearing snow sprites, and there were also husky dogs flanking her sides. The Queen wore a shimmering crown made from icicles and stars from the sky. Her crown of stalagmites sat upon her wild dark, hair and a flowing white cloak, trimmed with white fur, draped her shoulders. There was the special silence of snow present, and all that was heard was the tinkling of bells held by the snow faeries.

The Queen held a wand in her hand, tipped with a symbol like a snowflake, a six-rayed star shape that mimicked the snowflakes' appearance. She halted the procession and flicked her wand; at once a flurry of snow spun around her presence, whirling around the snow sprites.

The Snow Queen, mistress of yet another faerie portal, disappeared down her Snow Well, and I was left in a snow flurry, in awe of her magical and powerful presence.

The Snow Queen points us in the direction of our unconscious desires. Through her we see the creation of possibilities and dreams fulfilled. She is beauty and light and also treacherous danger and darkness, which are the characteristics of snow and winter. Work with her and you will certainly know it, for her energy is awesome yet also empowering.

She wishes to be known once more in her faerie form, instead of the misrepresented portrayals in literature and post-Christian folklore. Her message is love and transformation, for whatever she touches is changed forevermore. See her as the angel of the snow and a sparkling light in the darkness with her lantern and crown of stars.

Queen Mab

Queen Mab is also known as Medhbh and Maeve and appears in Shakespeare's *A Midsummer Night's Dream* renamed as Queen Titania. (Some also know Queen Titania as originally the Goddess Diana.) She is the best-known Faerie Queen and is generally perceived to be the Queen of All Faerie.

She began her life as a mortal, the Irish Queen Maeve of Connacht, although some sources cite her as a Welsh queen. It was believed that in her mortal life she enjoyed favourable relations with faeries, and for this she was rewarded with healing powers and spells. In her mortal reign she was highly regarded and also feared, as legends depict her as a warrior queen, winning battles with her womanly cunning rather than brute force. In her lifetime she was considered to be sexually insatiable, and the mere sight of her was reputed to take away two thirds of a man's strength.

Queen Maeve won her title as Queen of the Faeries through a series of battles, magic, bravery and strategy, making herself immortal. Also considered to be a faerie goddess, she is believed to be one of the first mortals to enter the legends of the Celtic faeries.

As Mab, Queen of the Faeries, her legends are many, and her name means intoxication. Many famous poets and

writers, including Shakespeare, have written about her. While writing this book, I sat down to attune to Queen Mab and receive a message from her.

Queen Mab's Impression

She chose to show herself to me in my little garden on a summer's night. She stood in the exact spot where I leave my faerie offerings. Her presence was awesome, and I really felt that my breath had been taken away for a moment. She appeared in a long white dress that shimmered and jingled as the fabric moved in the breeze, although I could not see any bells attached to it. She had long, sleek black hair and piercing faerie-slanted blue eyes. She was intensely and exquisitely beautiful, and her whole body seemed to be surrounded by an aura of shimmering white light, as if she was bathed in her own personal moonlight. She was also surrounded by flowers, predominantly roses. Everything seemed to be accentuated around her; the breeze sounded like a woman's whisperings and the air felt crisper and purer.

Mab, who traditionally illuminates our dreams and is the keeper of faerie magic, touched the back of my hand and smiled. I turned my hand over and opened my palm to reveal the key to my dreams and the unconscious.

She commands the surge of magical tides that go unseen, held in private half-awake moments. She wishes us to take more notice of the signs and symbols that our dreams send us. Messages sent via the ether are more subtle and take practice in reading and interpreting. Keep a dream diary, and Queen Mab will show herself to you in the undercurrent of your subconscious. Learn to meld your subconscious desires with your conscious will and you may resolve inner conflicts and be more at peace with yourself. Queen Mab can only help those who seek to find her and also those who dare to know.

Morgan Le Fay

Also known as Morgana, Morgaine and Morgan, Morgan Le Fay's name means 'Morgan the Fairy' and may be derived from the Welsh *mor*, 'sea', and *gan*, 'a birth', meaning 'born of the sea' or 'sea dweller'. Morgan in Breton means 'Fabulous being supposed to live under the sea'.

Morgan Le Fay's origins are more complicated than most. In one version she is said to have originated from the water nymphs of Breton folklore. These morgans are said to lure sailors down to their subaqueous palaces. They are known to be seductive and sexually alluring, attributes shared by Morgan Le Fay.

In her mortal life, her origins are also many. She is said to be the daughter of Avallach, King of Avalon. Other sources tell us she was one of the daughters of Gorlois, Duke of Cornwall, and his wife Igrain, of Arthurian legend.

All sources are resolute that in legend she was associated with Merlin and from him she learned magic, acquiring the skills of shapeshifting and the healing arts of herbs and balms. She was also sexually manipulative and known as a

siren in her time. She had many lovers, all of whom are said to have broken her heart. She is also said to be the half-sister of King Arthur and famous as the Queen of Avalon or Glastonbury Tor, the Isle of Apples, the Enchanted Isle, the magical island between the worlds, outside time and space. In Avalon she dwelled as mistress of the Sisterhood of Nine. Morgan Le Fay is associated with several goddesses and in some sources derived from them. Some authorities link her with the Irish goddess Macha, a warrior queen, and also Morrighan, another warrior goddess. She is also known as a goddess in her own right, a goddess of Avalon or Glastonbury and of sovereignty.

Morgan is believed to be one of the most celebrated of all the Faerie Queens, keeper of the portal to Faerie Land in Avalon and an enchantress who lures you to the hidden and magical depths in your mind.

I asked Morgan Le Fay for an impression of herself and this is what she sent us:

Morgan Le Fay's Impression

I was shown her standing upon the Tor on a blustery evening at twilight. The wind whipped around her billowing skirt and her arms were outstretched to the sky. She appeared to be completely in possession of her own power, and she looked like a compelling figure in the half-light. Her face was strong and determined, yet alluring and beguiling. She

was raven-haired and wore a necklace of apple pips around her neck. Her long dress was apple green and the fabric so soft, like gossamer, a cloth unknown to humankind. A golden chain lay around her hips, and from it hung a velvet pouch of magical herbs. Upon her fingers were rings inscribed with magical symbols. She stood in the twilight, as that is one of the most potent times to attune to faerie magic and enter the realms of the unseen. Glastonbury Tor, a doorway to Faerie Land, becomes stirred at dusk. Morgan Le Fay, Queen of the Portal, can help us to enter the faerie realm and also the hidden realms of the self.

Morgan is a bright illuminator, but also a dark mistress. She lures but also changes us, bringing a transformation through the darkness into the light. Some sources interpret her as a dark Queen, but she is dark with a spiritual purpose, plunging us into the dark waters of human emotion and intense sexual feelings and making our spiritual growth one of creative transition. You can only truly appreciate the light if you have known at least some darkness. So Morgan is our guide, the one who holds the lantern to our fears so that we may face them. To know this Faerie Queen intimately, you will have to journey with her and emerge on the other side.

More Queens of Faerie

Once you have recognized which Faerie Queen you are going to work with, you have an excellent starting-point from which to proceed on your pathway as a Faerie Priest or Priestess.

Of course there are many more Faerie Queens than I have illustrated here, and if one has already made herself known to you, try to find out as much as possible about her, as this will help you to work with her on a deeper level of understanding. To help you find a Faerie Queen who is suited to you, I have briefly included three more who may ignite your imagination to initiate contact.

Queen Oonagh

Also known as Oona and Una, she is the Irish Faerie Queen at the court of the Daoine Sidhe (pronounced 'Deena Shee') and is the wife of the womanizing King Finvarra. She is one of the Faerie Queens of the race known as the Tuatha de Danaan and is reputed to be the most enchanting and beautiful creature in the Land of Elves and the mortal world. She has the ability to shapeshift, but her most favoured form is that of a young calf.

If you would like to visualize Queen Oonagh, she has a slender faerie frame that is traditionally adorned with a silver gossamer dress which sparkles with glittering dewdrops. Her luxurious hair is golden and touches the ground. You may call upon her for help with enchantment and faerie magic, all aspects of beauty and forbearance in an unfaithful marriage.

Queen Caelia

Caelia is a Celtic/British Queen of Faerie and is also featured in literature in Edmund Spenser's *The Faerie Queene*. In British legend she enchanted the illegitimate son of King Arthur, the already married Tom a'Lincoln. They had a son together, a faerie knight named Red Rose Knight.

Visualize the beautiful Queen Caelia, and call upon her to help you with aspects of motherhood, faerie magic and enchantment, kindness and allurement.

Queen Argante

Argante is the Faerie Queen of Avalon and is connected with Morgan Le Fay. According to some sources, she and Morgan are one and the same, but others disagree. Her name means 'silvery one' and she belongs to the Elven race. According to Arthurian legend, King Arthur went to Argante in Avalon when he was mortally wounded in his last battle. Conflicting sources also connect Argante with the Welsh goddess Arianhrod, whose name means 'silver wheel'.

Visualize the radiant Queen Argante in a white or silver dress and call upon her for help with contacting the elves and working with them, healing of all kinds and faerie magic.

Your Faerie Queen's Guiding Light

Your Queen is essentially your friend and faerie mentor. She will be there to hold your hand on your journey of discovery in Faerie Land. However, just because you have the assistance of a Faerie Queen, do not expect your pathway to be easy or uneventful. Faerie Queens take us through the shadows as well as through the light, and only by travelling the whole journey of the self can we rightly follow the path of faerie.

Remember that the Faerie Queens demand respect, and if you ever forget this, they will be first to let you know. Allow her to enter your dreams and meditations, actively ask for her advice and talk to her about your spiritual direction. She will always be there for you, as a divine aspect of nature, but she can only really help if you ask for her assistance. Remember the faeries' vision is for humankind and faeries to work together for our mutual benefit, so your Faerie Queen will not mind if you ask for her guidance. Working with a Faerie Queen, I believe, is the ultimate privilege, and she will support you as you tread the path of faerie.

We all experience spiritual and emotional phases, so do not be surprised if after a period of months or sometimes many years, your Faerie Queen is replaced by another one. You may also experience working with more than one Queen at the same time at particular phases in your life or transitional times. This is all perfectly natural, and even if a Queen is no longer your faerie guide, she will always leave a profound impression upon your life and will be remembered fondly in your heart. Faerie Queens can also return to guide you after a time of absence, so I believe that once a connection is made, it is never forgotten.

If you wish to work with one of the three Queens I have focused on in this chapter, it can be very helpful to use the psychic impressions as a meditational starting-point. This can initiate meditation images of your own, and of course using the tool of your imagination will always bring you closer to the faeries.

6

The Throne of the Faerie King

The Faerie Kings and How to Work with Them

'Oberon: But we are spirits of another sort:
I with the morning's love have oft made sport.'

WILLIAM SHAKESPEARE,
A MIDSUMMER NIGHT'S DREAM

Who Are the Faerie Kings?

As with the Faerie Queens, the Kings have been described as demoted Celtic gods who were forgotten and faded into the realms of Faerie Land. Faerie Kings are too overwhelmingly numerous to list, especially those of the Tuatha de Danaan of Ireland, for there is an abundance of information regarding this race. This once majestic and powerful people, whose kings were afforded status as gods, eventually became the Daoine Sidhe and, according to Brian Froud and Alan Lee in *Faeries*, 'with the encroachment of Christianity ... they diminished in importance, they correspondingly dwindled in size to become a race of faerie beings'.

The tales of the Kings tell of lives interwoven with battles, lust and magic, and devotion to their fey Queens. Faerie Kings are the rulers of our dreams; they will take us on horseback to those enchanted places of our imagination that only a King can command us to unlock.

The Faerie Kings have many qualities which are beneficial to the seeker treading the faerie pathway. One of the Faerie King's natural traits is his will to protect his kingdom and people. As a faerie seeker, you work for the faeries in a very special and blessed way and for this reason the Faerie Kings will support you in your spiritual work and offer you protection and guidance. Although protection is their primary function, each Faerie King also has his own magical qualities which he brings forth.

As in the previous chapter, we will focus on three of these faeries to help you begin your working partnership. In time you will forge a mutual alliance with the Kings of Elfland.

How to Work with a Faerie King

Working with a Faerie King, as with a Queen, is the ultimate privilege and should not be ventured into lightly. Dabbling with any sort of faerie magic will bring undesirable results, if not sooner then later. This particularly applies to the Faerie Kings, who will not readily tolerate dabblers. A Faerie King will only communicate with you if your intentions are honourable and serious. Faerie Kings demand respect in all your dealings with them and are shrewd in recognizing those who are wasting their time. That said, to form a spiritual union with a Faerie King is a truly magical and intense experience.

You may already feel drawn to work with a particular King, and if this is the case you can begin to work with him straightaway. Building up to this gradually is a good idea, as the energy of the Faerie Kings is not on the gentle wavelength of some of the Queens. Find out as much as you can about your chosen Faerie King from books and folklore, so that you have as clear a picture of him as possible. Write him a letter and place it on your faerie altar or in the crevice of a tree root. Leave presents out for him in a special, natural place, such as your garden or by the side of a stream. (Always something readily biodegradable.) Write him some poetry; in fact, use anything that engages your imagination to connect with him. Anything that brings him into your world that works for you is great, for faeries connect to your sense of creativity.

Once you feel that the Faerie King has entered your consciousness in some way, then you may begin to meditate on him. Let him know that you are going to be tuning into him; tell him the time and place of your meditation and invite him to be there. Write him a poem or invocation, however short. The more effort you take in contacting him, the more vivid your results will be.

When meditating, simply ask the Faerie King to be with you, and you should begin to see meditational images. If you have trouble initiating images, begin with what you think your Faerie King looks like in your imagination. Alternatively, you can visualize a King you have seen in a book or a painting to kickstart the meditation. If you begin like this, then the images should naturally unfold. Do not worry if this takes a few attempts. Instant results would in fact be quite unusual!

Once you have become accustomed to meeting your Faerie King, then you may use your meditation encounters to further your relationship with him. For example, you can ask him questions, confide in him and ask him for protection. Do not expect your answers to always come directly from your meditation. A magical process rarely has straightforward results. You may get your answer in a book you read the next day, in a conversation you have with a friend or in any number of symbolic ways that your Faerie King knows that maybe only you will understand. Answers are threaded throughout life, and the Faerie King is there to point you in the right direction.

If you are not yet drawn to a particular King, or your knowledge is not yet wide enough to choose one, then you can still ask a Faerie King to work with you. Although this method can take a little longer than if you already know your King, as long as you have the desire to bring one into your life, then you will be successful. There is a Faerie King out there for you somewhere, you just don't know who he is yet! So be patient; these things take time and devotion. Think of the most important quality you would like your King to possess and ask that a Faerie King of that persuasion be made known to you. You may feel that you need a Faerie King to be strong, protective, wise, mirthful, especially magical or perhaps loyal. Use the same methods as described above to bring your Faerie King into your consciousness, but instead of using a name in your faerie letters, poems, etc., describe him with his desired trait, e.g., 'wise Faerie King', and he will be made known to you in some special way, maybe through a book, film, conversation, painting or lecture. You will know who your King is when you find him because it will just feel right. He will resonate with your being, and his name will feel magical. Once you have found your Faerie King, then you can begin to meditate with him as described above.

If you feel inspired to work with one of the Faerie

Kings outlined in this chapter, then visualizing the meditational impressions I have recounted will give you a good beginning in creating a vision of your chosen Faerie King.

King Finvarra

Finvarra is a King held in high esteem and a member of the Daoine Sidhe, the race of Faerie Kings who dwell within the hollow hills, mounds or raths as they are known, of Ireland. His particular abode is Cnoc Meadha (pronounced 'Knockma'), a great hill west of Tuam, Co. Galway, where there is also a burial mound.

Finvarra is also known as Finnbheara, Finnbarr and Fionnbhar. He is King of the Connaught faeries, but is also considered to be the High King of the Irish faeries, and in some sources he is also the King of the Dead.

This Faerie King is an interesting character, and there are many legends surrounding him. His father is Dagda, once known as the chief god of the Tuatha de Danaan and later a Faerie King. Once again, Dagda is a faerie whose origins are misty, and there are some sources that cite him as originally being a god of the Underworld and/or the Dead.

Queen Oonagh (or Una), Finvarra's consort, despite being the most beautiful woman to exist in either world, is unable to keep her King faithful, for Finvarra is renowned for womanizing. He especially has a liking for mortal women, and it is said that he uses faerie glamour to lure them away to be his dance partners in faerie rings and then charms them to dance the night away with him in his palace. However, by some faerie magic, these earthly lovers are always found safely asleep in their own beds the next morning.

There is a famous tale of a mortal, Ethna the bride, whom Finvarra lured to his mound. Her bridegroom was not so lucky and had to try for three nights to win her back

from Faerie Land. On the third night his persistence was rewarded, and the next morning his bride was discovered safely asleep in her bed.

110

Finvarra, as with many faeries, is also said to have a passion for horses. His own horse is black with flaring red nostrils. In one of my meditations with Finvarra, I received a vivid image which I would like to share with you:

As I plunged into a meditative state, the air became shimmery and thick and I heard tinkling bells on the breeze. Then Finvarra appeared on a highly strung black stallion of faerie blood. The horse pranced, pawed the earth with his hoof and snorted impatiently, not wanting to stand still. The animal seemed huge, much larger than a mortal horse. Finvarra himself wore an outfit of worn brown leather. His very presence was magnetic and awesome. He was ruggedly handsome with a gentle smile. He wore a black velvet cloak lined with scarlet, and his horse wore a saddlecloth of the same. He came with the energy of goodness, but it was also very evident that working with this Faerie King would require a little getting used to, as his energy was awesome.

King Finvarra's Impression

Despite my earlier experience, while I was working on this chapter I seemed to be having problems meditating with Finvarra. Although I was receiving information and images, I knew that these meditations were lacking in the vital ingredients: magic and vividness.

I was about to sit down and meditate one evening in an attempt to gain more compelling results, when I suddenly realized that meditating indoors for this Faerie King was all wrong. I absolutely had to be among nature. So on that occasion, a beautiful balmy May evening, I ventured out into my little garden with a blanket to sit on and my notebook and pen. Quite by 'chance' the time was dusk, one of the most favourable times of day for a faerie encounter. I was not to be disappointed.

As I sat down, it was as if the garden was greeting me and I was immediately aware of its consciousness. It seemed that everything was moving, every blade of grass, every petal, every stalk. I could hear the stalks creaking under the weight of their flowerheads, I could hear snails eating leaves and the plants actually breathing. I knew that I was experiencing a heightened sense of awareness and was feeling nature as a spiritual dimension. This was an encounter that I was being given, and I knew that I had been right to act on my impulse and venture outside. Learning to act on your impulses, your so-called gut feelings, the inner voice within you, is extremely important when working with the faeries and can take years of practice. Some people are better at it than others, but it usually takes a certain amount of inner courage because it is not always the answer you want to hear, or the easiest option.

I hadn't even managed to close my eyes to meditate, and already wonderful things were happening to me. I felt the noises of the traffic on the road outside fade away to a place that I didn't inhabit. The domestic sounds from the houses nearby seemed to be happening in somebody else's world, not mine. I felt that I was encircled by a faerie ring of a radius of approximately four feet. All was clear within that circle, but outside it was hazy and blurred.

I asked my faerie mentor, Queen Mab, to bring me protection and also to bring me Finvarra. I requested this by way of a little rhyme:

'To invoke Finvarra is my task.
Dear faeries, assist me in what I ask.'

Invocations need only be simple; it is the intent that is the key. As soon as I spoke this invocation, I felt an immense presence towering behind me. His hands were upon my shoulders, and I had a few moments of giddiness when it seemed my reality shifted and my heightened awareness became more profound. Finvarra was an imposing being behind me, and he seemed slightly taller than an average human man would be. I have often experienced the Faerie Kings and Queens as human-sized or slightly larger, which has surprised me, although any other faerie beings have appeared as anything from about eight inches to three feet tall in stature.

Finvarra's sense of wisdom and earthiness, almost as if he were made from the earth, is what was conveyed to me in feelings. His energy was definitely kingly, and his presence was an all-encompassing encounter.

As I sat in the garden, I began to perceive coloured lights prancing around the circle. I knew that the faeries were with me, and I felt as if I was truly having a magical encounter. Until that point I had felt a little in awe and slightly tense at being in the proximity of a towering Faerie King, but now I relaxed and felt relieved. The faeries around me brought with them a loving energy, and I realized that this was the vibration that Finvarra had also come with. It was as if I were among friends, which of course I was.

It also seemed very clear what Finvarra was all about: clarity. I had asked to experience King Finvarra, and I had been shown nature as it really was and how the faeries themselves experienced it – as another spiritual dimension with its own compelling vigour.

The whole twilight encounter brought to me a refreshing sense of peace. The garden had awakened my senses, both physical and spiritual, and I felt very honoured to have connected with this wonderful Faerie King. I closed my meditation by saying, 'Blessed Be' to my circle of fey friends and to Finvarra. I began to become aware of everyday sounds once again and went indoors as the dusk was succumbing to night.

<hr/>

King Oberon

This King is bound to British history almost as closely as Shakespeare himself. Oberon was of course adopted by Shakespeare to provide a faerie element in *A Midsummer Night's Dream*, where he became Oberon, King of the Faeries, to play alongside his Queen Titania. No chapter on Faerie Kings would be complete without including Oberon. However, his origins are far from straightforward, and we can delve behind Shakespeare's portrayal and unveil a myriad of Oberons. Shakespeare was in fact not the only

115

one to portray Oberon in literature. Ben Jonson wrote a masque about Oberon. Composers have also found inspiration in Oberon, and Weber named an opera in his honour. Many poems throughout history have also been dedicated to him. Oberon is still inspiring people today to write about him in poetry and creative writing, and there are numerous books and internet sites devoted to him.

As with most of the Faerie Kings and Queens, Oberon is presented throughout folklore in many varying aspects. One fact never wavers: he is always a Faerie King. In many sources, unlike Shakespeare's depiction, he appears as a dwarf king. This is true, for example, of the mediaeval French romance *Huan de Bordeaux*, where he is known as Alberon, the son of Morgan le Fay and Julius Caesar, and portrayed as the King of Avalon. In Germany he appears as Alberich, again King of the Dwarves. In contrast, in other stories he is described as an Elf King. His origins are thought to be Germanic, although many of his stories contain Celtic elements, with Oberon as a guardian of treasure or a magic cup. He is even celestial: one of the moons of Uranus was named after him. One thing remains certain: whatever his true origins, he has inspired creative individuals of many cultures to bring him to life through art forms. He is now definitely embedded within British culture, and whether you meet him as a dwarf, elf or Faerie King, his presence is legendary.

When tuning into Oberon, I chose his Faerie/Elfin King aspect, as this is the most popular image of him. It has already captured our imaginations and, our vision is the paramount ingredient when contacting a Faerie King.

King Oberon's Impression

When embarking on this meditative journey, I knew instinctively whom I should ask to assist me in contacting Oberon. When I sat down to meditate, the first thing I said was, 'Dear Queen Mab, take me to your Oberon,' and so she did. This is a perfect example of how your Faerie Queen can help you on your faerie pathway. Your Faerie King has the capacity to come to your aid in a similar way.

⌐⌐⌐

Queen Mab took my hand, and we came to an archway of creamy roses. There were rose petals scattered upon the grass. It was as if we were walking through a wedding archway. I felt that this archway was symbolic of Queen Mab and King Oberon's link with one another, as Shakespeare's Titania is Queen Mab renamed. I realized that I was barefoot, but Queen Mab wore cream silk slippers. As we walked under the archway she turned to me and dabbed flower nectar upon my eyelids with her forefinger. At once my surroundings began to swirl and shimmer. The air became thick and dreamlike. I also had the sensation that I was travelling, although my feet were firmly on the ground.

After a moment, things began to steady and when I opened my eyes Queen Mab had disappeared and I met King Oberon in a woodland den. We were surrounded by dense trees that were covered in ivy and dog roses, and there was a sweet honey scent in the air. I had wondered which Oberon would greet me – elf, dwarf or faerie? It is sometimes suggested that faerie folk appear to you in the guise that you expect or that you find most acceptable. You may or may not believe that, but I think it may be true that a faerie's appearance is in some way determined by our imagination. In Oberon's case, a collective imagination has been at work, due to Shakespeare and other artists transforming him from ugly dwarf to handsome King of the Faeries.

I was in no doubt that the Oberon I was in the company of was definitely elfin. His hair was fair and long, and he wore a small crown fashioned from vines which was decorated with suspended rubies and emeralds. The crown was cushioned on a circlet of moss upon his head, and as I peered more closely I could see tiny spiders weaving threads to suspend the jewels. This intricate activity transfixed me for a moment, almost a meditation within a meditation. Then my eyes moved down to his ears, which were pointy and virtually touching his crown. He appeared to be very youthful, with slanting elfin blue eyes, pale skin and full lips. His frame was slender and he wore few clothes. He told me that he celebrated the eternal summer and that his traits were a reflection and embodiment of the fullness of that season. His energy and appearance were in absolute contrast to those of Finvarra, for his presence was not awesome but mysterious, magnetic, intriguing and maybe even a little mischievous. His power is the magic of the imagination of creativity, summer sexuality and allurement.

I have often noticed that one of the gifts of a Faerie Priest or Priestess is to be able to lure people from one dimension to another. You can use it to help others to enter Faerie Land through meditation, dreams and astral travel, although always with the other person's consent and full knowledge. If you work spiritually with a partner, then this is the ideal employment of your gift. However, always be mindful of its pitfalls. This is a gift that can easily be mis-used and can obviously be applied to manipulate others. If in doubt, don't use it at all. Oberon would, however, be the perfect faerie mentor for this type of magical exploration. If you are a magical adventurer or require creative inspiration, then Oberon could be the King to align yourself with.

Gwyn ap Nudd

Gwyn ap Nudd (pronounced 'Neath') is a Faerie King who commands a very large stage as a Celtic ruler of fair Elfland. There is a wealth of information devoted to him and he is a prominent figure in British folklore.

Gwyn ap Nudd presides over two faerie kingdoms, one being the enchanted Otherworld Annwn, with its secret entrance in the Welsh Lakes. The Wild Hunt is known to ride out from the doorways of Annwn with Gwyn ap Nudd as their leader. The Wild Hunt is a sky-riding proces-sional host of hunters on magical steeds, followed by their hounds. Many places in the world have their own version of the Wild Hunt and differing Wild Huntsmen as their leaders. *The Illustrated Encyclopaedia of Fairies* by Anna Franklin tells us that 'they emerge from the Underworld

… and ride the storm'.

Gwyn ap Nudd is also King of a palace beneath Glastonbury Tor. There is a legendary tale of St Collen who once lived at the foot of the Tor. He refused many invitations to visit the faerie castle. Eventually he decided to take up the invitation, and armed with a container of holy water he climbed the hill to St Michael's Tower, was taken underground and entered the beautiful castle. There he found himself at a banquet where the guests were pretty maidens and handsome youths, troops of soldiers and servants all attired in red and blue. Gwyn ap Nudd was seated among the frivolities upon a golden throne, and he cordially welcomed St Collen to join in the merriment and partake of the food and drink. St Collen replied that he did not eat faerie food. The colours they wore of red and blue echoed the state of demonic fire and ice in Hell. He then took it upon himself to douse Gwyn ap Nudd and his company in the holy water, which made the King and his palace disappear. St Collen was left standing alone at the top of the Tor.

Another legend of Gwyn ap Nudd also centres around Glastonbury and its magical inhabitants. Gwyn is forever chasing the hand of the faerie maiden, the beautiful Creiddylad (cree-thil-aahd). She is supposed to have married Gwythr, however, Gwyn ap Nudd stole her away before the marriage could be consummated. King Arthur was called upon to officiate and he ordered that the two opponents should fight for Creiddylad's hand every May Day until Judgement Day. This spring contest is seen as a symbolic battle between the forces of winter and summer, at May Day, the cusp of the two seasons, for the hand of the earth goddess in her aspect as Creiddylad.

As a Faerie King, Gwyn ap Nudd rules over the Tylwyth Teg, also called 'the fair family'. They are small Welsh faeries with naturally fair hair and are recognizable by their white clothing. They also have the peculiar characteristic of only being visible by night.

Gwyn ap Nudd is also seen as a powerful King linked to Annwn, the place where the souls of the exceptionally blessed go after death. He is commonly depicted with an owl, also a symbol of death. When we speak of death in connection with Celtic deities, however, it is a different concept from Christian and other religions and cultures. Celtic societies did not give death sinister or dark connotations. It was seen as a transition to another place, where it was said to be always summer and where everyone enjoyed good health and happiness.

Gwyn ap Nudd has earned his reputation as a Faerie King of mysterious powers with mysterious ways, and to work magically with this King would be an honour.

Gwyn ap Nudd's Impression

Before I had even started to meditate, Gwyn ap Nudd had arrived. I was writing at my desk at that magical twilight time again and looked out of my window to the woodland beyond my house. There I saw the Faerie King riding over the treetops on a magnificent white horse with a flowing mane and tail. I realized that this was how he would appear as head of the Wild Hunt. Generally speaking, in folklore it is considered a very bad omen to see the Wild Hunt or hear it flying overhead. I have witnessed the Wild Hunt on two occasions, however, and it was not an unpleasant experience. They were definitely beautiful, spiritual times of extreme heightened consciousness, when

I even witnessed giant snowflakes falling in my bedroom. I sensed no feeling of foreboding, only love, freedom and delighted wonderment. For both times I witnessed the Wild Hunt it was at the conception of babies and on both of those occasions I later lost them. I still cannot say why I had these experiences, but the presence of the Wild Hunt was a comfort, as there was a sense of a divine plan in motion. The faerie realms come to us at all times of our lives, bringing a celestial presence particularly at the bringing in and departing of souls from this life.

Now I watched Gwyn ap Nudd fly towards my house, and behind him was a trail of speckled lights, glimmering as if they were stardust over the glistening trees. He was dressed all in green with a fur around his shoulders. Upon his head were antlers mounted on a copper crown. He was a rugged, bearded figure with the darkest, deepest eyes I have ever seen. In one hand he held the reins which jingled like sleigh bells, in the other hand he held up a sword that had a handle woven in leather with a Celtic design. The sword was highly polished, and he brandished it skywards as if he were about to go into battle.

When I had finished my writing, I went downstairs to meditate. As it was a full moon at twilight, I was hoping for vivid results. As I closed my eyes and tuned in, I was immediately transported to the summit of Glastonbury Tor, where I found myself wearing a long moss-green dress. I was standing alone until opposite me there appeared Gwyn ap Nudd, dismounting from his exquisite moon-shining faerie horse.

The Throne of the Faerie King 123

I was taken aback when the Faerie King bowed before me and proceeded to take my hand and gently kiss it. He then presented me with a crown of small antlers, which he placed upon my head. He mounted his horse once more and pulled me up behind him into the sheepskin-lined saddle. I put my arms around the King's waist and held on tightly. He smelled of earth and moss. The horse suddenly took flight, and we soared over Glastonbury and the countryside surrounding Avalon. He showed me many hill formations and told me that these were the hollow hills of the Sidhe. He said that he guarded them and cloaked them with faerie glamour. I felt very protected and safe with him, which is something that surprised me.

As the dusk was drawing into darkness, he said that we must return to the Tor. The horse alighted on the soft moist grass and I slid from its back. Gwyn ap Nudd seemed to fade away, and I was left standing alone on the Tor.

If you are in need of protection and direction on the deeper things in life, the aid of Gwyn ap Nudd may be the answer you are seeking.

More Kings of Faerie

If you do not resonate with any of the three Kings illustrated above, there are of course many other fine Faerie Kings to work with. To help you find a Faerie King to suit you, I have briefly included three more which may spark your interest to find inspiration.

King Sil

Silbury Hill in Avebury, Wiltshire, is reputed to be the highest prehistoric man-made mound in Europe and according to legend is named after the Faerie King Sil, or Zel, whose name means 'great'. It is claimed that King Sil is buried within Silbury Hill, either upright on the back of his golden horse or in a golden coffin. According to Robert Graves in *The White Goddess*, Silbury Hill is 'the original Spiral Castle of Britain', making this site a place of power. Some believe it to be a faerie portal to Elfland and the afterlife.

If you would like to visualize King Sil, local folklore says that he still rides around the hill on moonlit nights wearing golden armour. He is a powerful Faerie King guarding the gateway to Faerie Land and the realms of death over which he is known to have power. Call upon him for help with transitions in life and gaining entrance to Faerie Land.

King Donn Fierna

The Irish Faerie King Donn Fierna is lord of the faerie mound Knockfierna. His name means 'dark one' or 'black one' and he is reputed to live on an island situated off the south-west coast of Ireland called Tech Duinn, 'the House of Donn'. This is an archway through which the sea flows, and it is a gateway to the Underworld where the dead begin their journey to the Otherworlds.

If you would like to visualize King Donn Fierna, he is said to ride out on black stormy nights on his white faerie horse. Donn rules the Otherworld and the Land of the

Dead. Call on him for help with faerie magic, protection and powerful aid with problems which may seem overwhelming, for he is a great force.

King Midar

Midar, also Midhir or Midir, was once an Irish god of rebirth, but dwindled in significance to become the Faerie King of the Tuatha de Danaan. His story is that he fell in love with the Irish mortal Queen Etain, or Edain, and snatched her by means of enchantment from her husband, the King of Munster, Eochaid. After a long pursuit by Eochaid, Midar released the enchantment upon Etain and she was able to return to her dear husband.

Call upon King Midar for help with faerie magic and anything relating to a complete change in life.

Your Faerie King's Guiding Sword

As my meditational journey with Gwyn ap Nudd illustrates, faeries are known to inhabit the hollow hills, or mounds, of our land. Each hollow hill is presided over by a Faerie King and Queen, but the fey inhabitants usually owe their protection and loyalty to a High King. A Faerie King's most prominent trait is therefore protection, and an alliance with one of them is a wonderful and also sensible relationship, especially when you are starting out on your faerie pathway. Just like the Faerie Queens, they will be your friends and mentors.

If you wish to connect with Finvarra, Oberon or Gwyn ap Nudd then you have a head start, as you can use the psychic impressions given here as starting images for your own meditations. Seeking the right Faerie King can be a magical pathway in itself, and you will not usually find him at the place or time you expect. These are the Faerie Kings you are working with, so be prepared for the journey you didn't foresee!

128

7

Away with the Faeries

Reaching into Faerie Land with Meditation

'"Come dance with us, sweet nature's child,"
she heard their voices sing.
For lost was she to mortal man,
within the faerie ring.'

STEVE FOX,
THE FAERIE RING

This Way to Faerie Land

Meditation is the most important tool when connecting with the faeries. There are two reasons for this, one being that meditation is accessed through the spark of your imagination. Your vision is the number one ingredient in building a relationship with the fey people. When in a meditative state, you reach out to the astral planes and communicate with the faeries on their wavelength. Faerie Land is separated from our own world by a veil of consciousness. It is a place where thought manifests as form. So when you are meditating, you are behaving in the very same way that faeries naturally function.

I firmly believe that the imagination is a real place, as real as the place where you are reading this right now. Just because something does not inhabit our fourth-dimensional reality does not mean that it cannot exist. Things often start off in your imagination and become 'reality' at a later date. This book is living proof that your imagination is real, as since the age of 11 I have imagined myself writing books, and here I am! Your mind visions have an impact on your physical reality as well as being another reality all of their own.

This leads us to the second reason why meditation is important, as your imagination partly exists in the Otherworld, the astral world. Faeries are of course astral beings, and Faerie Land is an astral place with connections to our world. Meditation enables us to embrace both worlds through the imagination, which inhabits them both. Therefore your imaginative meditations will create a sparkling astral bridge of light that will empower you to visit faeries and their land.

I am not talking here about the kind of meditation where you are required to concentrate on nothingness and empty your mind for 30 minutes. This type of meditation is of course extremely valid and I have practised it myself, but here we're going on a journey with a specific destination, which means that we need parameters. For this we use the type of meditation that is known as *pathworking* or sometimes *guided meditation*. For clarity, I will use the term *pathworking*. This type of meditation takes you along a prescribed route, unfolding like a story. It works very much like listening to or reading a story from a book. Just as words in a book create pictures in your mind, so in a pathworking you visualize images as the story emerges. A pathworking is a meditation template for you to follow, a safe framework within which to venture into Faerie Land.

Once you have become practised in this method, you can create your own pathworkings by writing them down or even taping your own voice so that you can listen to the pathworking and follow it without having to remember all the details. After a while you may discover that you have favourite pathworkings which you like to meditate on regularly or when you are in need of inspiration or faerie assistance. I have included three of my own favourites at the end of this chapter. I like to visit them again and again, like a special old book or film. In this way they can also provide comfort or reassurance in times of need, as you are connecting with faerie, an essence of the God energy. The three pathworkings I have included are also excellent for the fledgling faerie seeker, as they take us through three very different methods to begin a pathworking. I hope that they will inspire you to create your own pathworkings. I can help you to begin your meditative journey with faeries, but I can only take you a short distance along the faerie pathway. It is of course your own input that will achieve the most magical results, as *your* imagination and not mine is the key.

Pathworkings do not always have to be totally directed. On many occasions a pathworking will take you on a meditative journey to meet a particular faerie or find a special place and you will be left to fill in the visionary gaps.

Creating a Castle of Dreams

Meditation is naturally comfortable for some people, while others find it an uphill struggle at first. The common thread for everyone, whether you find it fairly easy or downright difficult, is that it involves practice and dedication. Not many people will receive fantastic images and messages the first few times they meditate, for meditation is a skill that needs to be cultivated and that requires regular disciplined commitment. Throughout this chapter I will provide guidelines on how to meditate safely and effectively and also suggest a meditation structure.

To meditate you need to become aware of your etheric body and to feel comfortable with your own body's energy centres. We have orbs of energy all around our body and it is also surrounded by a field of lights and energy called the aura. At the moment we only need concern ourselves with

133

the seven main energy centres, which are known as chakras, a name deriving from the Eastern spiritual systems. I will refer to them individually by their Western names:

> The first chakra is situated at the base of the spine and appears as a red orb of pulsating light; it is called the base chakra.

> The second is called the sacral chakra and is situated at the sacrum level of the pelvis. The sacral chakra resonates as an orange-coloured light.

> The third chakra is situated around the solar plexus and can be visualized as a yellow orb of light.

> The fourth energy centre is in the middle of the chest and is known as the heart chakra. This is seen as a green sphere of vibrating light.

> The fifth chakra is known as the throat chakra and can be visualized as an iridescent centre of blue light.

> The sixth energy centre is the third eye chakra and is situated on the forehead, in between your physical eyes. This centre can be seen as a spinning violet light.

The seventh chakra, which links you to the heavens and higher forces, is the crown chakra at the very top of your head. This is seen as a pulsating orb of celestial white light.

Before you begin to meditate or indeed embark on any kind of magical work, you need to activate your spiritual body by opening your chakras. This also means that when you have finished meditating, it is imperative that these psychic centres are closed down. You also need to finish with a grounding exercise, which I will explain further on.

It is essential that you take care of your energy centres, as these are your doors to the Otherworld. If they are left open, it is akin to leaving your front door wide open onto a busy street, an open invitation to anyone who may be walking by, and an attractive opportunity to undesirables. The same applies to your chakras being left open. You want to attract only those beings and faeries that you invite to contact you, and you also want to work with those that function at the highest possible vibration and light.

When you are first becoming aware of your chakras, you will begin to notice if they are open or closed. As you start to work with them, you should become more sensitive to your etheric body, and the more you practise opening and closing your chakras (as outlined below), the more attuned you will become to their well-being and vibrations.

Before you begin the meditations in this chapter, it is a good idea to practise opening and closing your chakras. Do this over a number of days or even weeks, it really doesn't matter, whatever your own personal schedule allows. The most important point is to practise regularly, as your chakras are like psychic muscles – the more you exercise them, the more flexible they will be.

Sensing Orbs of Light

Here is an exercise which you can use to safely open and close your chakras. Don't be put off by the length of the exercise on paper; after you have practised it a few times, you should be able to open and close your chakras in less than 30 seconds! However, in the beginning this procedure should not be rushed. You need to take time to familiarize yourself with the exercise and also to get used to the different sensations of each chakra. If you are doing these exercises with a friend, so much the better, as you can help each other to sense your chakras. It is of course perfectly fine to do this exercise by yourself.

Opening Your Chakras

There are many different ways to open your chakras, and I have been taught several. However, the following method is the one I have felt most comfortable with and the one that has stuck. I teach this method to my apprentices, although in time everyone finds the approach that suits them best.

Begin by choosing a time and place where you will not be disturbed. At first this exercise will take you 20 minutes to half an hour, but of course with practice you will need a lot less time. You also need to make sure that there are no distractions; put the answering machine on and a polite note on your front door. If you have small children, make sure you choose a time when they are at nursery or soundly asleep. This is your time to connect with the faeries. Let them know beforehand the day and time when you will be doing the chakra exercise and they will be waiting for you and your results will be more productive.

You need to make sure that you are warm and comfortable and sitting in an upright position. This can be on a chair or on cushions on the floor, whichever is most comfortable and convenient to you. Your arms and legs should ideally be uncrossed to allow energy to flow freely throughout your body.

I always light a green candle when I am doing any kind of magical work with the faeries. It creates a special atmosphere and takes you out of the everyday. You can also burn your favourite incense or oil on a burner. Always make sure that naked flames are well away from curtains, etc. while you are concentrating.

Chakras can be opened from crown to base or from base to crown; the following is the method I prefer.

Close your eyes and concentrate on your own stillness within, the place where the real you resides, the you that doesn't have to pretend to be anything to anyone else. Find that place and take some long, slow, deep breaths. Imagine breathing in pure white light and breathing out sparkling white light.

Once you have done this a few times and begin to feel relaxed, say a short prayer, either silently or aloud, to your faerie mentor. If you do not yet have a special mentor, then simply address your prayer to 'Dearest Faerie Queen/King' or to your guardian angel. You need to address this prayer to a faerie or celestial deity that you believe will bestow protection on you. Request politely that they protect and guide you in this exercise.

Then imagine a neon blue ribbon of light swirling around your body, starting from your feet and wrapping a protective ribbon of light right up to the top of your head. The blue light should twirl clockwise around your body. Once it has reached the crown of your head, imagine this shielding light is tying itself in a bow above your head to ensure your psychic safety.

Now you can activate your chakras! First of all you need to imagine a pool of white light in the ground directly beneath your base chakra. You are in control of this light. It belongs to you as universal energy, to which everyone has access. Shoot this white light like a spurt of water in a beautiful fountain up through your body, through the pathway of your chakras and out of the top of your head via your crown chakra. This light is aiming to reach the heavens and the purest point of your imagination. Visualize there the King and Queen of Faerie, splendidly attired and bathed in white light. Imagine yourself there with them and they will greet you with an embrace or a kiss, or both. While you are with them, ask them for their protection and also for their guidance with this exercise. If you have any other concerns or needs while you are with them, then tell them while you are there.

Leave the Faerie King and Queen in the heavens and shoot down the same celestial fountain of white light to the crown of your head. This is where you get to be creative, as visualizing your chakras is a very personal thing and most people like to envisage something that has meaning to them. Some people see the chakras as spinning wheels of light, others as trapdoors with padlocks of the appropriate chakra colour. As I work with the faeries, nature-based beings, I visualize my chakras as enormous flowers. For simplicity I will describe the opening and closing of the chakras in this way, but of course you are free to experiment with your own ideas. As a general guide, visualizing anything that naturally opens and closes will work well, such as doors, lids, portals, windows, etc. See what you feel most inspired by and comfortable working with, and then stick to it.

Imagine an exquisite flower in bud at the crown of your head. Slowly and carefully imagine the bud opening and the petals unfurling to reveal a beautiful white flower. From that flower shines resplendent white light. You have now opened your first chakra. Note the sensations it produces.

Send the fountain of white light a little way down your head to reach the bud of your third eye chakra. Again imagine the petals unfolding out, this time to reveal a violet flower from which violet light is pouring out.

Once you feel comfortable with this energy centre, shoot the white light down further to reach your throat chakra. Visualize the bud unfolding into an iridescent blue flower, much like the blue of a kingfisher bird. From this chakra comes glorious blue light.

Moving down the body again to your heart energy centre, you find this bud reveals a lovely green flower from which a sparkling green light flows.

Shoot the white light downwards once more to your solar plexus chakra, where the bud unwraps itself to become a bright yellow flower, rather like the strength and beauty of a sunflower.

Imagine the white light flowing down from your solar plexus to your sacral chakra bud. This bud unfolds to become an orange flower with orange light pouring from the centre.

Finally, shoot the white light down to its final destination, the base chakra. Open the waiting bud out to reveal a vibrant red flower with strong red light emanating from its petals.

To conclude this exercise, imagine that you are looking at your chakra-lit body with all its flowers pouring light from their centres. The flowers should appear healthy and in their prime; the light needs to be flowing strongly from each chakra. If any of the lights are weaker than others, then concentrate on visualizing them as stronger and more vibrant. Everyone has particular chakras that are more difficult to open than others and you may feel more at ease with the energy of some chakras than others. This is natural, and by regularly opening and closing your energy centres, you can learn to balance your chakras. As your body lightens up, chakras are a reflection of your overall physical, mental, emotional and spiritual well-being. If you are upset, for example, you may find it difficult or even painful to open your solar plexus chakra. If this kind of phenomenon occurs, then it is best to leave that chakra alone until you feel better. Ask your faerie mentor for healing to be sent to you and to that particular place.

You should fairly quickly become sensitive to your chakras and how they respond to opening. If you find a certain chakra difficult to open, ask for help from your faerie mentor there and then and visualize opening that chakra again. Asking for assistance usually brings guidance straightaway, but be sure to listen to the answer, and, of course, your own intuition.

This completes the opening of the chakras exercise. If you were going to embark on a pathworking, you would follow on from here. Similarly, if you were creating a faerie ritual, you would start from this point. All magical work requires your energy centres to be alive, as they are your connection to the spiritual realms and, of course, the faeries. Once you have completed your magical work, whether it be a pathworking, ritual, spell or special ceremony, then you will close your chakras again.

Closing Your Chakras

It is vital that your chakras are closed down after you have opened them, as you risk your health if they are continually left open. Closing them is a simple exercise and much shorter than the opening method.

Begin by reaching your imagination up to the heavens, above your crown chakra. Visualize the Faerie King and Queen, who greet you with a kiss. Ask for their blessing and protection on your closing and bid them farewell by saying 'Blessed Be.'

Shoot your beautiful white light down to your crown chakra, see the white flower and carefully close the petals to form a green bud. Some magical practitioners recommend that the crown chakra should not be closed at all, as it is the portal for spiritual energy from the heavens. However, I was always taught to close this chakra, but leave it slightly ajar, and from personal experience I feel that this is wise. If you are a very sensitive and psychic person, leaving it totally open can cause problems. Leaving it slightly ajar is a sensible compromise which has always worked well for me. In fact even if you attempted to completely close your crown chakra, you would probably not be able to do so. Nature intends to keep you in touch with the spiritual energy of the heavens, so do not fret too much over this issue.

Bring your white light down to the violet flower of the third eye chakra. Visualize closing the petals to form a tight bud.

Once you have completed this, send your white light downwards once more to your throat chakra. Close the petals of the blue flower to form a bud.

Shooting your white light now further down to the green flower of your heart chakra, close the petals firmly shut until they are a green bud.

Then bring the stream of white light down to meet the yellow flower of your solar plexus chakra. Close this flower firmly until it is a little green bud.

Send your white light down further to the orange flower of your sacral chakra and bring the petals to a close.

Finally send the white light to the last energy centre, the base chakra. Again there are differences of opinion as to whether to close this chakra, as this is the orb which allows the Earth's energies to flow through. Indeed, when

I was first training, the medium who taught me advised me never to open this chakra at all. However, when I began a wiccan pathway I found this chakra was routinely used because wiccans work directly with Earth and sexual energies, both of which are governed by the base chakra. For the base chakra then, I apply the same principle as with the crown chakra and leave it slightly ajar, so that energy may still flow freely through. By doing this, you are still generally guarded from unwanted negative energies. Close the red base chakra flower to form a loose bud.

Now visualize your body with its central line of chakra buds. You may be able to see if any of the buds have popped open again. This sometimes occurs. If this has happened to you, then double back and close the chakras that have popped open. If a particular chakra persists in coming open, ask for help from your faerie mentor. Pathworking with a friend is good as they can 'manually' close your chakras down by placing their palm on them and visualizing along with you the chakra in question closing. This is an extremely effective method and usually has rapid results. If you are working on your own, you can also 'manually' close your chakras by placing your palm on the chakra concerned and at the same time asking for assistance from your faerie mentor. I always close my chakras with the manual method as a matter of course, as I find that way they are less likely to pop open later.

Once you have closed your chakras, then you need to conclude with a simple grounding exercise.

Feet Firmly on the Ground

A grounding exercise is extremely important to bring all the energy you have been utilizing into the earth. Very often even after properly closing your chakras, you may still get a 'spaced out' feeling. This is because of residual energy. So performing a grounding exercise is a sensible routine to get into. It should follow closing your chakras as naturally as brushing your teeth before you go to bed!

There are many grounding exercises that are effective in earthing residual energy and I recommend three of them here. All of these are universally used by magical practitioners. You can use them in isolation or one after the other. You can't be too grounded!

From Your Head to Your Toes

This exercise works on the principle that all energy needs to return to the earth and the earth will absorb it, like a neutral substance, rather like an earth wire in an electrical plug.

Stand up straight, but relaxed.

Beginning from the top of your head, brush in a downwards direction with the palms of your hands, as if you are brushing dust from your clothes. Imagine you are brushing the residual energy downwards into the earth.

When you reach your feet, visualize the energy draining from your toes into the absorbent earth.

Once you have finished, firmly hold your feet. This feels extremely earthing. If you are working with a friend, then holding each other's feet in turn is even better and has a very reassuring and grounding feel-good factor.

Quick Grounding

If you do not feel particularly in need of a grounding exercise but simply want to make sure that all the energy has been earthed, then this exercise can help:

Simply clap your hands a few times, quite hard.
Then stamp your feet on the ground very firmly.

This is an instant earthing exercise and useful if time is a factor.

Feeling the Earth

This is the most thorough of the three grounding exercises in this chapter, and I always use it myself after I have completed any magical work.

For this exercise you need to be sitting down, preferably on the floor. If that is not possible, then a chair is fine. Visualization is the key to this exercise – and of course your imagination!

Imagine that your body is the trunk of a tree. You are a being of the earth and belong to that element. In place of skin, you have bark and within your veins you feel sap flowing instead of blood. You are home to many creatures, whom you welcome into your boughs.

Now focus on your feet and imagine that they are your roots. Feel them extending into the earth. They are strong healthy roots and reach deep down into the ground. Feel the earth around your roots. Imagine the damp smell of the soil and all the creatures that dwell in the earth. Imagine that your roots are curling around rocks and large stones in the earth, so that you are really firmly anchored to the ground. You can take as long as you need to visualize and sense your root system. You need to feel that you are part of the earth and that is where you belong.

While visualizing your roots, you can also repeat the words 'I am strong' either mentally or aloud. This reinforces your sense of strength and groundedness.

Once you feel sufficiently grounded, then you can slowly visualize yourself with a human body once more, open your eyes and come back to everyday reality.

After any kind of magical or meditation work, you should make sure that you eat and drink something. Drinking pure water especially cleanses the chakras, and eating food helps to close the energy centres. By putting food, a product of the earth itself, into our bodies, we are physically bringing ourselves back down to earth. Even if it's just a piece of toast, you need to make the effort to put this into your meditation routine. If you are meditating with one or more friends, then this can turn into party time! Well, any excuse, of course, but the faeries would certainly approve, as revelling is one of their favourite pastimes. Have your party in honour of the faerie folk and they will be very pleased indeed, as long as you remember to leave a small offering from the feast on your faerie altar.

Beginning to Meditate

Once you have become comfortable with opening and closing your chakras and using grounding exercises, then you can begin to meditate. A short pathworking, something around five minutes long, is the best way to begin.

Meditating needs to be practised regularly if it is going to become an effective method for you to reach the faeries. However, you know the realities of your own life and what you can fit into your day. When you are starting out, it is best not to meditate more than once a day, as you are still getting used to the new energies you are using. If you can fit in one pathworking a day, that is ideal, and you would be doing very well if you could follow that meditation routine. If you are experiencing pathworking on a daily basis, your connections with faerie will blossom extremely quickly. Meditation is definitely an activity which adheres to the principle 'the more you put in, the more you get out'.

The most productive time of day to meditate is first thing in the morning. If you have a busy family life, this may be the most advantageous time to find a quiet space, before the house comes alive and the day carries you away with it. Of course we all have our own routines, and first thing in the morning may not be the best time for you. The most important factor is that you find a time of day that suits you and stick to it. Remember, once you have become familiar with your chakras and meditating, it will only take 15–20 minutes a day.

If you can only find the time to meditate once a week, then so be it. But whatever your routine, if you want results, then you need to keep to it. You may want to keep to the same pathworking every time for a while or you may like to try a different one every time. The choice is yours.

Meditating Safely

If at any point during a pathworking you feel anything unpleasant or you get an uneasy feeling, then open your eyes immediately. Just forget meditating for that day and cut the pathworking short. Make sure you close your chakras as usual, perform a grounding exercise and eat and drink something. These are usually one-time events and everything should be fine next time you come to practise your pathworking.

However, if this should happen to you on a regular basis, say more than three times, you do need to examine the cause before you can continue. Make sure that you are always asking for protection and visualizing the blue ribbon of light. If you are depressed or going through a particularly stressful or negative time in your life, it can manifest in your pathworkings quite easily. This is your unconscious mind reminding you that something in your life desperately needs to be sorted out.

If this is the case, then you need to take a step back. Take a break from the faerie seeking and pathworking for a while and go and sort out your emotional/physical/mental/financial life. Your spiritual life will only flourish if the rest of your life is more or less balanced. Of course most people will have more than a few problems and that's part of life, but if they are affecting your spiritual development, that's the faeries' way of communicating to you that you need to look after yourself first and foremost. The faeries will be there waiting for you when you are ready to resume your spiritual pathway.

Pre–Pathworking

Once you have time to yourself, you have followed the chakra-opening routine and you are sitting peacefully, here's how to prepare for a pathworking.

First of all, breathe deeply and focus on achieving as relaxed a state as possible. Meditation is an altered state of consciousness where our brain enters the alpha state, the place between waking and dreams, which is rather like Faerie Land, the place between this world and the next. Deep relaxation is the key to entering this state.

Meditation is a skill that is opposite to how you are in everyday life, for it requires you to actively focus inwards. It is an extension of daydreaming if you like, but focusing on one specific thing. Mind wandering will not help you to meditate and the inner noise of your own constant thought stream has to be controlled. So meditation is a discipline, yet it is also a freedom. Allowing yourself not to be reminded what you plan for dinner tonight or to wonder whether you really remembered to put the rubbish bags out frees you from your everyday state and lets your mind and soul freefall in a very different and explorative way.

Silencing inner distractions can be the most challenging aspect of learning to meditate. The most trivial and annoying thoughts will venture into your head when you thought you were doing so well. Persistence is the only way to learn the skill of inner focusing, but your reward will be the awakening and flowering of your unconscious mind.

You may already have your own relaxation method which works for you. If not, you might like to try this approach:

Become aware of your physical body. Beginning with your feet and toes, you are going to tense your muscles for a count of 10 seconds.

Crunch your toes up and tense your feet. Really concentrate on feeling the tension in your feet and toes. After 10 seconds, let this tension go, breathe it out and allow your feet and toes to become floppy and relaxed.

This tensing and relaxing method carries on up your body. Tense each part in turn for the count of 10. Go up to your calves and knees, then your thighs. Now tense your pelvic region, now your torso and chest. Move on to your fingers and hands, then to your forearms, elbows and upper arms. Your shoulders and neck will be next and then your scalp. Move onto your face and tense each feature in turn: your forehead, eyes, cheekbones, nose and teeth, lips and jaw.

You may be amazed at how this method leaves you tinglingly relaxed.

Once you have completed this relaxation exercise, you are ready to follow your pathworking. I have devised four short pathworkings for you to try. Try them on separate occasions, not all in one meditation session. You may like to read one aloud and tape it, then once you are ready you can play it back and follow it without having to remember it. If you are working with a partner or in a faerie circle group, you can take turns to read a pathworking out while the others follow it.

These four short pathworkings are about the elemental faeries. They will introduce your etheric self to the concept of the four elements and how each one will affect you. Working with the four elemental faeries will attune you to the essential spiritual elements of air, fire, water and earth.

The Elemental Pathworkings

These four pathworkings all take place in the same woodland and are all interconnected. Once you feel comfortable with them in isolation, you can try all four together, linking them up so that one follows on from another, making a complete elemental journey.

The Sylph Pathworking

Imagine that you are in an English woodland with many varieties of trees. There is a pathway wending its way through the trees, flanked by moss and trailing ivy. The time is midsummer and the woods are at their most lush and vibrant.

Follow the pathway into the woods. You are completely alone and the only sounds come from the birds singing, insects buzzing and your own footsteps. Take in your enchanting surroundings as the late afternoon sunlight dapples on the green leaves and the pathway.

After a short walk along the footpath, you come to a pleasant clearing. A fallen tree lies here amidst an array of wild flowers. The tree trunk is luxuriantly covered in moss, so you may take a seat there. Sitting down, you can watch the many butterflies which are fluttering and flitting among the charming wild flowers. You sit for a while, taking in the fresh air and watching the butterflies in the beautiful clearing.

After a while one butterfly in particular catches your attention. The sunlight seems to catch it most mysteriously, almost as if it is surrounded by an aura of golden light. You become very interested in this particular butterfly and focus upon its movements. Sometimes it flits very close to you and you can actually see it taking nectar from the flowers. It is a red admiral butterfly and the patterns on its wings are incredibly detailed.

Suddenly your special butterfly comes to land on the mossy tree next to you. Although you have seen no actual transformation, it appears that it was not a butterfly after all, but a sylph faerie. He has the exquisite wings of a red admiral and the slender body of a butterfly, but he is definitely faerie. He is slightly furry all over his body and face and his eyes are velvety black. He blinks a few times and definitely looks at you as if he has something important to say: a message perhaps, or a question. A breeze rustles around the trees and the woodland clearing, the sylph faerie takes off to join the other butterflies and now, quite strangely, becomes indistinguishable from the other butterflies tending the flowers.

You get up and retrace your steps back to the footpath. As you walk along the track, you wonder what the faerie wanted to say to you. Perhaps you will find out when you visit the clearing once more. When you have reached the end of the pathway, come out of the woods and into the sunshine. Now you can open your eyes in your own time. Your pathworking is completed.

The Salamander Pathworking

Imagine that you are in the woodland once more, but this time following a different footpath. This is a steep pathway carved into a hill. The uphill walk is made easier by some steps made from wood built into the earth at intervals. You begin by following the steps and the sun beats down, as this pathway is less shady, being at the edge of the woods.

As you reach the top of the path, you see a stable and a barn. There are two chestnut horses in a meadow beyond, grazing contentedly. Outside the stable you notice a small smouldering bonfire where stable waste and dry hedge clippings are being burnt.

The smoke spirals upwards into the sky as if it has a consciousness of its own. This catches your eye and you stop and watch. The smoke seems to be spiralling in the most peculiar and beautiful patterns, quite unlike any smoke you have seen before. This entrances you and you sit down on a tree stump to watch it.

After a few moments you begin to see a form within the smoke. It is a long, thin tapered faerie form. Its limbs are lithe and seemingly flow into the rest of the smoke.

Suddenly you become more aware of the breeze; it is accentuated in your mind and senses. It must have been there before, but you do not recall it. You think you hear tinkling bells on the breeze, but you cannot be sure where they are coming from. It is a smoke salamander. Your attention focuses on the smoke salamander once again and she seems to be dancing to the faerie bells on the breeze. She is enjoying every moment of it and you take pleasure in observing her. As she dances her body elongates and then comes back to its original shape (such is the nature of smoke) changing its form continually. She seems to be aware that you are watching her. Your senses are heightened and you are experiencing the natural world in a timeless bubble of bliss.

After you have watched the smoke a while, the faerie fades and the smoke once again spirals with no particular form. You turn and retrace your steps down the wooden stepped hillside until you come out into the sunshine outside the woods.

Your pathworking has ended and you may now open your eyes when you are ready.

The Undine Pathworking

You enter the beautiful woodland on a fine midsummer's day. As you do so, you hear a lovely woman's voice singing in the distance and you are instantly drawn to it. You begin to follow the woodland pathway in the direction of the entrancing singing. The song sounds joyous and full of feeling and you have never before heard a voice so exquisite. You long to find out whose it is.

As you make your way along the footpath, all sound seems to be accentuated. You notice the birdsong more than ever before, the rustle of the breeze among the trees and the bees buzzing among the wild flowers. You pass the clearing where you sat with the sylph butterfly and continue on your journey. All the time the voice seems to be getting louder and you believe that you must be getting nearer to the singer.

Quite suddenly you turn a corner and find yourself beside a still pool. The water seems cool and inviting, and you realize that the singing has faded away. You sit down beside the woodland pool. There are dragonflies skimming the surface of the water, their shimmering bodies catching rays of sunlight. You take your shoes off to feel the cool damp moss beneath your feet and it is a pleasant experience.

A dragonfly skims very close to your feet, which makes you look up. You immediately notice a very beautiful young woman sitting on the opposite side of the pool. She could almost be human, but there is something a little fey about her. So striking is this feeling that you feel honoured to be able to see her. She sits on the wet moss as you do, but she is naked, with a pale slender body, almost tapered at the ends. Her hair is the most amazing sight, for it is black, wavy and luxuriant and reaches down to her knees, draping most of her body. A little frog sits beside her. She seems to be talking to him and he seems to be listening. You do not think that she has noticed you until she looks up from her *tête à tête* with the frog and gives you a little smile. She then slips effortlessly into the water and disappears, apart from her hair, which splays out on the surface of the water. You reach out to try and touch a thread of it and feel water weed slipping through your fingers. With faerie glamour, she has become her element.

Feeling as if you have witnessed a very special faerie, you leave the poolside and retrace your steps to the pathway. As you walk back along the footpath you begin to notice things that you don't think were there before: little coloured orbs of light in the trees, spiders' webs glistening in the sun and a feeling of the consciousness and interconnectedness of nature.

After a magical walk you reach the end of the pathway and emerge into the sunshine, bringing an end to your pathworking.

The Gnome Pathworking

As you enter the woods, you notice a magnificent tree. It is a glorious old oak with twisting vines and ivy growing all around its wide trunk. Its roots spread out, spanning the earth all around it and giving a sense of expansion and security. Such is the friendly nature of the tree that you feel invited to sit beneath its majestic boughs.

You sit down on the cushioned moss-covered ground with your back leaning against the trunk of the tree. This in itself is a pleasant and peaceful experience and you are lulled into repose by the tree's serenity. You enjoy the relaxation that being in the company of the oak brings.

Gradually the tree becomes the centre of everything, the only thing that matters in your slumbering mind. After a while you feel a glowing warmth next to you. You look down to see an orb of amber light, glowing and pulsating by a thick root. Slowly the light fades and in its place, still surrounded by an aura of amber light, stands what you instantly recognize as a gnome. He is about six inches tall and wears a moss-green jacket with matching trousers. He wears no shoes and his pointy hat is also green. He has a kindly face and of course a beard, which is very fluffy and more like the 'old man's beard' which blows off trees in the autumn than a human beard. He seems to be very preoccupied with sewing a blanket that appears to be torn in the middle. The blanket is made from leaves, all sewn together with minute stitches, intricately worked.

You watch him for a few moments sewing his little faerie stitches. He seems to be concentrating so deeply on his task that he is completely absorbed, almost as if it were a meditation. You also become drawn into the methodical sewing and it makes you feel as though you are completely in his world. You wonder if he is aware of you sitting next to him. As if in reply to your thought, he looks up from his sewing, smiles and nods you a greeting. Then the orb of amber light around him begins to shimmer and glow. It pulsates for a moment and then suddenly disappears, as if it were a bubble that has burst.

Your faerie bubble has also burst as you find that with the gnome's disappearance the woods appear normal again. The tree no longer dominates everything and seems to be just an ordinary tree. You get up and walk out of the woods into the sunshine, your pathworking now complete.

Pathworkings Spiralling to Faerie Land

Now that you have become practised at elemental pathworkings and you feel comfortable with meditating and entering the faeries' realm, you are ready to venture onward to pathworkings which bring deeper levels of the meditative state.

The elemental pathworkings used the backdrop of an English woodland, which is a physical place and familiar to many of us. Now you move to pathworkings designed to carry you to Faerie Land. They approach the Land of Elphame through three different doorways. There are many paths to Faerie Land and each of us will find our own way there. Use these meditations as inspiration for eventually creating your own pathworking portals to Faerie Land.

You may use these pathworkings on their own or, when you have read the chapter on faerie rituals, you can incorporate them into a ritual to enhance your fey experiences.

Remember never to dance, eat, drink or say thank you in the faeries' realm. When you have completed your pathworking, closed your chakras, grounded and feasted, then do not forget to leave a gift on your altar to show your appreciation.

The following pathworkings will take approximately 20 minutes to half an hour to complete. If you are working solitary, then taping the pathworking beforehand would be a benefit, but is not essential.

The Snow Queen's Procession

For this pathworking you may wish to burn a white or silver candle in honour of the Snow Queen instead of the usual green one. Prepare yourself as usual by opening your chakras, visualizing your protection and going through your relaxation exercise. You are now ready to follow the Snow Queen to the place of dreams.

~⁓~

You see before you a field at twilight covered in virgin snow. In the field is a mound, or hollow hill as it is known, and beyond that are snow-covered woodlands. It is the night of the full moon and the stars shine sharply in the darkest blue sky. The snow glitters in the moonlight as the sky slowly creeps to black. You stand all alone in the tranquil surroundings.

When it is completely dark, you begin to walk through the snow towards the hollow hill, leaving deep footprints as you go. You are dressed warmly, all in white.

As you approach the hollow hill, you see something sparkling and glistening next to it. It seems to be transparent and quite beautiful, and if you are not mistaken it is a sleigh. It seems to be a solid object and is one of the most beautiful and engaging sights you have ever beheld. Sparkling around it are coloured lights that appear and disappear in the darkness. You recognize them as faerie lights and you feel in a very magical and special place.

The faerie lights gravitate to the ground before your eyes. As you watch them, they begin to transform into faerie beings, lantern-bearing snow sprites.

Away with the Faeries 161

You have hardly had time to take in this astonishing sight when you hear the sound of excited dogs playing and barking in the woods next to the field. You can also see the bobbing and swaying of a large lantern being carried through the dense woodland. The snow sprites around the sleigh start to chatter excitedly and gather upon the glistening sleigh, lighting it up with their tiny lanterns.

The dogs seem to be drawing nearer, together with the luminescent lantern. At last you can just about see through the darkness of the trees who the lantern-bearer is. You recognize the Snow Queen herself, Holda, grasping a long spiralling stick with her magic lantern suspended on it. The lantern seems to emanate a silvery white light, quite unlike a candle flame. The queen is tall and slender and has bountiful dark hair which reaches in cascades of curls to her knees. She wears a striking white dress with a fur-edged train at the back which glides across the snow, creating a swift swishing sound. She also wears a heavy white velvet cloak with a fur-trimmed hood. Her face is animated and vivacious. She is a beautiful creature with a twinkle in her bright blue eyes and a smile on her red rosebud lips. She comes with a kindly energy and being in her presence feels magical.

When the Snow Queen reaches the sleigh, her pack of husky dogs gather quickly into their respective places at the front of the sleigh. They do this without fuss, as if they know exactly what is coming next. The snow sprites buckle the dogs into white leather harnesses. The Snow Queen gestures with her hand for you to get into the sleigh. You sit down on the sheepskin-covered seat and she seats herself next to you.

You have a feeling of excitement and suspense as everything feels so enchanting. All at once it begins to snow in moonlit flurries and you are transfixed by the falling flakes. As though that were the cue to begin, the Snow Queen rings a little bell on the sleigh. At this sign the dogs begin to pull the sleigh swiftly and smoothly across the snow meadow. They are enthusiastic in their endeavours and seem to be enjoying every minute. For you too the sleigh ride is a joyful experience; the breeze flies through your hair and the sleigh is lit up by the many tiny lanterns which the snow sprites hold. It is an exhilarating experience. You sit back and revel in the fun of it all.

Then the Snow Queen rings the little bell once again and without warning the sleigh glides up into the air, the dogs pulling it upward into the starry sky. The Snow Queen whoops with delight and, like you, seems to be enjoying the whole journey immensely.

Your ascent becomes steeper as the huskies climb higher into the clear night sky. The flurries of snow still whirl all around the sleigh, even though there appear to be no clouds. It is as if this were the Snow Queen's own personal snowfall that follows her wherever she goes. Although you are high in the winter sky, you do not feel the slightest bit cold, but surprisingly warm.

The snow flurries seem to be getting more intense, and for a few moments you cannot see where you are going. Then the snow whirls suddenly disperse and everything has altered. You seem to have entered another place. You are travelling over another landscape entirely. The woodlands are no longer English, but Scandinavian forests of tall spruce trees, topped with caps of snow. The landscape is dramatic and the countryside expansive.

The Snow Queen rings the little bell once more and the huskies begin to descend into a clearing in the forest. You cannot see exactly where you are going to land, but you do see hundreds of coloured faerie lights twinkling below. After a few moments it becomes clear that you are heading for a glorious lantern-lit frozen lake in the middle of the dense forest.

The sleigh glides gracefully and smoothly down to land on the ice. As you look around you, you realize the place is utterly enchanting. There are hundreds of snow sprites bearing lanterns around the perimeter of the frozen lake. In the centre of the ice is a gorgeous faerie altar, decorated with swathes of white velvet, tiny white flowers and lanterns emanating the same silvery white light as the Snow Queen's lantern. At the centre of the altar are two icicle crowns. One is large and ornate and rests on a circlet of white velvet. Eight snow sprites glide over and, taking hold of the crown, place it on the Snow Queen's head. She kisses them all and they seem to find this very amusing and giggle a lot! They then glide to the smaller, more intricate icicle crown. This time they place it on your head. With this gesture you have been honoured by the faeries and granted entry into their realm. The Snow Queen kisses you on both cheeks. Her kiss is not cold, as you would expect, but extremely warm, so warm that you feel filled with love.

She climbs back into the beautiful sleigh with you by her side and rings the tiny bell once more. Suddenly a flurry of whirling snowflakes encompasses you both, the huskies and the sleigh. It is not an unpleasant experience and you can see the pattern of each individual snowflake as they swirl before your eyes. For a few moments, there is nothing except glittering snowflakes. Then you hear the little bell once again and the flurry subsides. Although you had no sensation of travelling anywhere, you are now sitting in the sleigh in the field next to the woodland where you set off. The Snow Queen is standing next to the sleigh with her lunar lantern, surrounded by her excited huskies. She smiles and blows you a kiss and then begins to walk into the woodland, disappearing a few moments later. The snow sprites take your hands and guide you out of the sleigh. You step out and take one last look at the enchanting faerie sleigh.

Your journey to the faerie realms is complete. Bid the sprites farewell and when you feel ready you may open your eyes.

Take a few moments to reflect on your pathworking and then close your chakras thoroughly, complete a grounding exercise and make sure you eat something.

If you feel so inclined, it is often a good idea to write down your experiences and feelings about your meditation journey. Meditations are like dreams – they will feel very blurry by the next day, however vivid they are at the time. For this reason, if you want to record your pathworking, writing it down pretty much immediately is essential.

The White Faerie Mare's Spiral

This is my favourite pathworking of all time, and I often find it very comforting to use. I think this is because it creates a completely tranquil encounter and I personally find it a healing experience in itself. I hope you find it a wonderful pathworking too.

For this pathworking, burning a white candle is appropriate. Prepare yourself as usual by opening your chakras, visualizing protection and performing a relaxation exercise. Faeries are traditionally associated with horses, as are witches, especially white horses. This mare will take you to Faerie Land, and she is to be treated with immense respect.

Imagine that you are standing at a gate which leads into a meadow. The time is midsummer and it is dusk. The meadow is full of long grass, bespeckled with wild flowers, buttercups and clover. In the centre of the meadow is a white mare. She has a flowing mane and tail and her white coat shines under the moonlight. You watch her as she grazes for a few moments. She is completely at peace and is an enchanting sight. The mare wears a white velvet bridle and the reins hang loosely around her withers. Attached to the reins are many tiny bells.

After observing her for a while, you climb over the five-barred gate into the field. You are wearing light summer clothing and your feet are absolutely bare. Before you reach the mare you stop at a cluster of daisies. You feel an impulse to make a daisy chain, so you sit down in the long grass and become absorbed in the activity of splitting the little stalks and threading.

When at last you complete the daisy chain, you look up to see that the mare has wandered over to you. You stroke her soft white muzzle and it is like velvet to the touch. You say, 'Hello,' and pat her strong white neck. She appears to be very friendly and loving, and as a special gift you give her your daisy chain by placing it over her head.

You spend a few moments patting, stroking and generally becoming acquainted with the mare. She has a wonderfully gentle and wise energy about her, and you feel relaxed in her presence.

When you feel that you are comfortable with her, you gather up the velvet reins and climb upon her bare back. The evening has waned to night now, and the full moon's light leaks gently into the meadow and dapples through the trees that surround the field. It is a good, safe feeling being astride the horse as you hold the reins and look across the meadow as the grass and wild flowers sway in the breeze. You suddenly become aware of the elements and feel as if you are experiencing a heightened state of awareness. Each second is a minute, each minute is an hour and you are very mindful of the breeze. It is a soft, light breeze and very pleasant on this warm summer's evening. You feel the breath of the wind running across your face and body and you see it ruffle the horse's long white mane. It tickles your toes and makes you feel alive and free. That is where the white faerie mare wants to take you, not to a place, but to a feeling. She is aliveness,

Away with the Faeries   167

the embodiment of a free spirit. Let her take you to the place where your spirit can soar. Succumb to the sensations of freedom and be totally and utterly in the bliss of tranquillity and oneness with nature.

The bells on the reins tinkle beautifully in the fine breeze and the mare begins to walk slowly and deliberately in a large clockwise spiral. She seems to know exactly where she is taking you. Trust her to take you on the journey and just relax into the experience. Take in the enchanting stillness of the night and as the mare walks in her spiral, feel the tips of the long grass touching the soles of your feet. This is a sensory journey, and your body is attuning itself to the small and beautiful details of the meadow and the mare. Feel relaxed and in control, feel the breeze, the grass on your feet, the moonlight on your eyelids, hear the bridle bells tinkle. This is all for you. Care not where you are heading, but drink in the experience of the moment.

The faerie mare is treading a spiral in the meadow, but also a spiral in the universe. She is treading the dream, taking you from one world to another through the portal of your senses. Everything feels calm and you may feel a sense of bliss and oneness with the universe.

The mare's steps start to become smaller as her spiral brings her to the centre of the meadow. You begin to see small winged faeries surrounded by light dancing on the spiral path that she has trod. You also notice that the spiral pathway has made the grass a darker green than the rest of the field.

Once she has reached the very centre of her spiral, the faerie mare stops walking. The stillness of the meadow and the night touch you and you begin to feel lulled by the whole experience. You feel safe enough to lie back on the mare's body and close your eyes. For a few moments you can freefall and just listen to your senses and the calmness within. With your eyes still closed, feel the breeze on your face and the measured breathing of the horse beneath you. Feel held by the universe in these moments. Your body is safe with the faerie mare, so let your spirit wander in the tranquillity. I will leave you for a few moments to be a part of the experience alone.

The white faerie mare nods her head gently, causing her bells to ring. This brings you back to the meadow and to your-self. You open your eyes and sit up on the mare's back.

Once you are comfortable and ready, the mare begins to retrace her steps back along the spiral. You feel relaxed and refreshed as you let her carry you on the spiral pathway.

Continue to take in your surroundings as she treads the pathway. You are becoming aware that the mare is no ordi-nary horse. It feels as if she is a faerie queen in a horse's body, as if you are being carried by an aspect of the goddess, a beautiful being for whom your spiritual well-being and happiness are the utmost concern.

Soon the circle becomes more expansive, and as it does so you feel more and more alert and less aware of the micro-cosm of the sensory world.

The mare eventually halts at the meadow gate, and you pat her neck and reluctantly slide down from her back. You stroke her muzzle and kiss her forelock before you climb over the gate to end your pathworking. The faerie mare wanders contentedly back into the depths of the meadow and grazes once more at the nucleus of the spiral pathway.

～⌒～

When you feel ready you may open your eyes and become accustomed to the everyday world again. Take a few moments to recollect your pathworking and then thoroughly close your chakras, work through a grounding exercise and eat and drink something. Remember to leave a gift on your faerie altar and write your experience down straightaway if you feel so inclined.

Opening Your Faerie Wings

The following pathworking is designed to give you the freedom to travel anywhere in Faerie Land.

Light a green candle and make yourself as comfortable as possible in an upright position, either on the floor or in a chair. Open your chakras, go through your protection and relaxation exercises and then be prepared to transform.

～⌒～

I want you to imagine that you are walking towards a misty green veil. You are quite safe and no harm will come to you. Proceed towards the green veil, made of the finest fabric you have ever seen, and push your way through it. You will find yourself in a beautiful place belonging to fair Elfland.

A serene garden awaits you. Here there are many varieties of roses, all in full bloom. Lavender bushes adorn the perimeter of the lovely garden and you can tell that the garden is regularly tended. All the elements are represented here: there is a small ornate pool with a white cat sitting at the edge and occasionally tapping the surface of the water with her dainty paw, there are garden lanterns with flickering candle flames around the pool's edge, there are little ornate windmills turning in the breeze and there are smooth pebbles and crystals at the pool's edge. The elemental faeries are hidden, but this is their place and they will assist you in your work.

Today you require the help of the sylph faeries of the air. In your mind, call upon them politely to assist your pathworking. Ask them to be with you in this winged meditation.

After you have done this you may feel their presence in the garden. If you do, then in your imagination reach into your pocket, where you will find a feather. Place the feather by the windmills as your acknowledgement of the faeries and your offering of thanks.

Imagine that you are sitting down on the grass by the little windmills. Take a few deep breaths of the sweet-smelling air and concentrate on being really relaxed. You are going to focus on your own body. Imagine a lovely green light surrounding it. This light raises your spiritual self to a higher vibration and brings you more in tune with the garden and all of nature.

Now focus on your skin. Imagine that it is sparkling all over, as if a faerie had painted you with rainbow glitter. Now you are a being that resonates with the beauty and magic of the garden. Visualize them enhancing your psychic awareness and making it possible for you to metamorphosize.

Now focus on your back and visualize a green bud on either side of your shoulder blades. These buds are bursting with life and you can see and feel them quivering, waiting to unfurl. They contain your faerie wings, but before they unfold you need to decide how you want them to appear. You may feel drawn to grow wings fashioned from gossamer thread, dainty and easily carried by the wind. Alternatively, you may desire wings which align you to a particular insect or bird – a butterfly or moth, for example – or the feathered wings of a blackbird or dove perhaps. The choice is yours, but each of these wing types comes with its own special energies, and you need to feel comfortable with your own wings' magical personalities. Choosing wings that you feel especially drawn to and can imagine easily is important, as they will become part of your own etheric body.

Focus on your wing buds once again and then visualize your wings, crumpled and damp at first, slowly emerging from the bud kernels. Use your mind and will to move them. Unfold them fully, so that their span reaches out to the very tips. For a few moments, let them be still to dry out in the breeze and the sun. Take this opportunity to really feel that they are a part of your etheric body. Feel the weight of them on your back and imagine you have sensations in them. If you have feathered wings, you can feel the breeze ruffling through your feathers. If you have insect or gossamer wings, you can feel the sun drying them out and making them firm and taut, ready for flight.

Once your wings have dried in the sun, extend them skywards and reach the tips to the sky. Go on, give them a stretch! Feel how beautiful you are with wings and sense the opportunities and freedom that they give you. Feel free to embellish them. If they are butterfly wings, give them a pattern, for example. Let your vision have no boundaries, for these are your wings and they are the embodiment of your freedom in every sense.

You need to become accustomed to your faerie wings and also the way you body feels with them extended. Give your wings a ripple. Flutter each in turn and watch them too, feel happy at their appearance. Be joyful to own faerie wings. Flap them about as much as you like and have a good giggle at the same time if you want. Really revel in the experience.

When you have had enough of exercising and playing with your faerie wings, then it is time to put them away for now. In future pathworkings you may eventually fly with them, when you feel that the time is right. However, you need to become fully accustomed to their sensations before you do.

Imagine your wings are folding up very tightly into the wing buds until all you can see are the green buds on your back. Dissolve the green light around your body and brush the glitter away with the palms of your hands. Bid the garden farewell, stand up and walk towards the green veil. Once you have walked through it, you find yourself back in the everyday world.

When you are ready, open your eyes and close your chakras firmly. Complete your grounding exercise and eat and drink. Remember to leave a gift out for the sylph faeries on your altar.

This pathworking is one that you can expand upon each time that you use it. Next time you may like to take a walk with your wings around the garden and experiment with feeling emotions through them. After a few pathworkings of getting used to your faerie wings, you can eventually fly with them to different destinations in Faerie Land. However, this is not as easy as it sounds, even with imaginary wings, so work up to it gradually. Remember to use protection and then you can have a lot of fun and insight with this pathworking.

Stepping Stones to Faerie Land

Pathworkings are stepping stones to Faerie Land and also a discipline to incorporate into other faerie experiences. They can be used in celebratory and magical rituals, at times when you need comfort and upliftment or when you are in need of guidance or faerie help. They are a powerful way of making your journey to Faerie Land an all-encompassing experience and a definite asset on your faerie pathway.

8

The Faerie Temptress

Who Is the Faerie Temptress, and Where Is She Taking Us?

'For you have strayed from the well-travelled way
Down a tangled path no other sees,
And followed the sound of my plaintive song
That sighs and whispers through the trees....
These many years I and my kind
No longer mortal step have trod
And we live outside of time
Betwixt the worlds of men and gods.'

DOMINIC WILLIAMS,
'THE FAERIE TEMPTRESS'

Who Is the Faerie Temptress?

Many years ago, at the beginning of my faerie quest, I felt a bit lost. I felt that I was a witch, but with a definite faerie element. However, I didn't seem to fit into a category and there wasn't any kind of name for the role that I felt I was fulfilling.

One day I happened to be looking at a very wonderful book on faeries and a page devoted to the 'faerie temptress/ enchantress' leapt out at me. After reading further, I realized that I was not a spiritual enigma after all, thank goodness. It was official: I existed.

The term 'faerie temptress' is a very archaic one and is not really in use today. However, it does conjure up beautiful and evocative images of Celtic ladies dressed in mediaeval garb, all good stuff to kickstart the imagination – just the realm we want to cultivate. The faerie temptress was once a lady exactly as described, but through the ages she has evolved. Now, I believe, she has developed into the Faerie Priestess or, as Doreen Virtue describes them in her book *Earth Angels*, 'Incarnated Elementals'.

The faerie temptresses or enchantresses of old were not actually faeries, as their name suggests, but mortals. However, through the study of magic and herbs, they acquired skills usually associated with the faeries and worked magically with the fey realms. Modern faerie temptresses still do. They are characteristically given protection from malignant faeries and often have spiritual experiences of faeries, very often in childhood. In short, they devote their lives to the elfin ways and sometimes wish to be a faerie or even secretly believe that they come from the faeries in some way or are a faerie in human form. Others believe that they possess faerie gifts and traits. In legend, it is said that after a lifetime of behaving like faeries and visiting their realm, temptresses do become faeries. In the meantime, they often take on the role of ambassadors of the faerie world.

'Now what about the men?' I can hear you thinking. Faerie tempters and enchanters do exist and generally the same principles apply to them as to the temptresses. Historically, they seem to have been a rarer breed. However in modern times it seems that Faerie Priests are following very closely behind their Priestesses when it comes to proliferation.

Faerie temptresses and their male counterparts are often thought to be faerie messengers in human form. They are regarded as humans with a faerie destiny. Could this be you? For the two years preceding the writing of this book, I took a workshop entitled 'The Faerie Temptress' throughout the UK. During my travels with the workshop, it became very obvious that there are lots of you out there who are so drawn to the fey folk that you feel they are a part of your being in some way. Many workshop participants came up to me afterwards to tell me of their amazing faerie experiences.

So, though you would be forgiven for thinking that faerie tempters and temptresses were lost in Celtic legend, my email is being bombarded by these lovely creatures, all wanting to find out about other faerie seekers like themselves and looking for information about working with faeries. So if all this faerie tempter/temptress stuff rings a bell with you, then you are certainly not alone. They are making a comeback, and there is good reason for this. As I mentioned earlier on, the human race is undergoing a spiritual transition at the present time. I believe that the tempters and temptresses are here to help the faerie race build a relationship with us for our spiritual and ecological benefit.

I wanted to use the terms *faerie tempter/temptress/ enchanter/enchantress*, even though they are outdated, because they conjure up an imaginative image. The word *temptress* also has a sexual connotation. Working with faeries does sometimes involve working with sexual energies. However, these temptresses wish to tempt you somewhere else and in this case it is Faerie Land.

I do believe the faerie tempters and temptresses are the historical counterparts of the Faerie Priests and Priestesses that we have today. These origins really show us that to be a faerie seeker is a kind of vocation. It is a deep inner knowing that not only shapes our ideas but also our identity and appearance. I have often noted that people who feel drawn to the faeriecraft pathway are very fey in appearance themselves. This phenomenon is something which currently, to my knowledge, remains unexplained. Are these individuals fey-touched in the womb, at birth, or even at their conception? Perhaps many generations ago their ancestors were part of a faerie/human marriage. These were thought to be common when relations between humans and the fey people were more integrated than they are today. These questions remain unanswered for the moment, but it is a fascinating subject and makes me think there is more to a Faerie Priest or Priestess than simply an interest in the fey.

In legend the faerie temptress traditionally wore black, violet, green or red, all faerie colours. In folklore it is said that she must follow the natural diet of the 'Ladies of the Forest', which is drinking plain water and herbal teas, and must never eat the flesh of creatures residing in the air, water or earth. In modern-day terms, this does sound excessively strict, but probably meant that temptresses followed a vegetarian diet and did not pollute their bodies with alcohol or anything that might be harmful to their system. Indeed, the modern Faerie Priest and Priestess often have sensitive bodies and delicate constitutions. This is because their bodies are finely tuned to the natural world by working with the faeries, and anything that is unnatural or has a lower/denser energy due to being slaughtered affects every part of their being.

However, this does not paint an exclusive picture, since you may be a Faerie Priest who is drawn to gnomes in particular and expresses earthy traits, drinks beer and enjoys pig roasts. The elfin world embraces all the aspects of faerie and so do the Priests and Priestesses. I have a friend who at one time had a faerie being who lived in the cupboard under the stairs. His staple diet was Guinness and digestive biscuits, which they left out regularly for him. So, as you can see, faerie folk are extremely varied and for every type there is sure to be a Priest or Priestess to match.

In legend the faerie temptress is portrayed as incredibly beautiful, tall and slender with large eyes. Morgan Le

Fay and Vivienne are famous examples. Faerie tempters are thought to have large eyes and a faerie feature or two. They are reputed to be hauntingly handsome and poetic. Examples of historical faerie tempters are Tam Lin, a mortal knight enchanted by the Faerie Queen and taken to live with her as her lover, whose story is related in the Scottish folk ballad of that name, and Robin Hood, the hero of English folklore who famously robbed the rich to give to the poor. His connections with faerie and magic are legendary. Doreen Valiente, in her *ABC of Witchcraft Past and Present*, mentions 'Robin Hood's band in Sherwood Forest … of twelve men and one woman, Maid Marion'. This is the sacred 13, a number regarded as having magical properties. It links Robin to faerie, as do his associations with the English deity Robin Goodfellow and his folklore links.

All these figures are reputed to have once lived mortal lives with close affinities to the faerie race and their magic. They are now faerie monarchs or faerie beings and inhabit the other realms, carrying on the magical work they began in their human lifetimes.

The Role of the Faerie Priest and Priestess

If you feel called to help the faeries, your journey will be a magical one, you can always count on that. Your faith can carry you through difficult times, and if you help the faeries, they will bestow upon you something wonderful in return. These faerie gifts are rarely material goods, but

gifts of special talents, a youthful appearance or healing for instance. The faeries will certainly bless those who befriend them and will help them in their own magical and unique ways.

The role of the Faerie Priest and Priestess is very much like that of the traditional witch. They live among ordinary society. They do not segregate themselves as a monk or a nun would do in order to carry out their spiritual work, but participate in the real world with all its pleasures and pains. In fact, it is important that they do live lives grounded in the real world, as their quest is so Otherworldly that they need the anchor of the mundane life to maintain a balance.

There is also another good reason why the Priest and Priestess do not shut themselves away in Faerie Land. It is that they are human representatives for the fey worlds and to assist the faeries they need to be active in the human world. They will often find that friends and relatives, even friends of friends of friends, will come to them for magical help or advice. It may be a request for healing or for advice on meditation, on how to rid their house of an unfriendly elemental or on how can they safely help their children to honour the faeries too. The Faerie Priest and Priestess will be asked to help others at the most unexpected times and often by the most unlikely of people. And the faeries will help, if asked, of course.

As well as helping others in a quiet and unofficial way, Faerie Priests and Priestesses all have their own spiritual journey to fulfil, and through this will eventually find their own niche, be it healing, spells, meditation or astral travel.

The role of the faerie seeker is also to listen carefully to the needs of the fey people. These may be expressed through the guidance of their chosen Faerie King or Queen or via elfin messages from pathworkings. However it is done, the faerie seeker will be guided on how best to help the faeries, and it is not always what they envisaged doing either! However, their own needs will not be forgotten. Sometimes, by acting upon guidance, you eventually realize that your needs have been met very well indeed, not as you may have imagined, but in the faeries' wonderful knowing ways. The faeries will not let you down, once you have decided to befriend them.

The Faeriecraft Dedication

If you do feel that your life has an enchanting meaning, that of helping the faeries, then you may like to take this one step further. Performing a faeriecraft dedication confirms to yourself and also to your faerie friends that you embrace the magical pathway.

This is not an initiation and should not be treated as such. A formal initiation is not necessary in faeriecraft, unlike traditional witchcraft, as the faeries specialize in their own magical initiation, tailor-made especially for you and delivered when you very least expect it! A dedication is for your benefit, illuminating your faeriecraft pathway in your own psyche. It will inevitably open more faerie doors for you to explore and give you the confidence to call yourself a Faerie Priest or Priestess.

If you feel that you would like to perform a faerie dedication, then I have included one below for you to use. You may follow it as set out here or you may feel you want to take the parts you feel inspired by and create your own dedication. The choice is all yours and you should feel completely comfortable with the rite.

This is something that it is a good idea to plan and look forward to. You may even decide to do it with a friend or maybe in a group of like-minded people. If you do decide to do this with others, then do make sure that you feel really at ease with everyone involved, as this is a very personal magical act. If you feel at all uncomfortable with anyone in the group, opt to perform the rite by yourself, as ultimately the dedication is between you and the faeries.

The best time to perform your dedication is on the night of the full moon. If it is really impossible to arrange this, then any night of a waxing moon, that is, the moon when it is growing to full, would also be appropriate. Always work with the natural tides if you can, as this will maximize any magical work. This may also be your first rite in faerie-craft, so make it something special and definitely something to celebrate. Make sure you put the night of your dedication in your diary, so you can keep it free and ensure no one will disturb you, and try to prepare as far ahead as possible.

Get something really special to wear. As this will be your first night as a Faerie Priest or Priestess, having something unique to wear is important. When performing any rituals, you should wear something that is only kept for that purpose. By keeping a garment specifically for ritual and magical use, you symbolically take yourself to the Otherworlds whenever you wear it and do not bring the taints of the everyday life into your magical work. It may be a garment that you already own, or you may choose to buy something new or even make something yourself. In faeriecraft you are limited only by your imagination of course, so even if you use an existing garment, you may like to customize it with embroidery, brooches or braids, for example. In witchcraft it is customary for priests and priestesses to wear robes and sometimes cloaks as well. In faeriecraft robes are also appropriate for magic, and choosing a robe in one of the faerie colours of green, violet, red or black would be fitting. However, if you prefer a beautiful long mediaeval-style dress, a Scottish kilt or anything else that you feel comfortable in, then that is fine. As long as that garment is kept only for your work as a Faerie Priest or Priestess, then it will be suitable.

Prior to the dedication, take a candlelit bath and soak away your everyday tensions. You may like to add a sachet of herbs to your bathwater to make this a magical cleansing time. You can do this by cutting a small square of muslin, then adding equal parts of any of these herbs, or just one of them if you desire: chamomile, lavender, rosemary, thyme and hyssop, and also a little sea salt. Bring all four corners of the muslin square together and tie it up with a piece of string or embroidery thread. Hang the sachet from your tap while the water is filling and then relax in your bath 'tea' and focus your mind on your dedication. All the herbs I have listed are suitable for any pre-ritual cleansing, but if you have sensitive skin, always test a patch of skin beforehand to make sure you will not react adversely to any of the herbs.

After your cleansing bath, dress in your robes or special clothes. Keep your hair loose, as unbound hair is a faerie trait, abundant with life force and free-flowing magical energy.

Where you hold your faerie dedication is also a personal choice. As long as you can be assured of absolute privacy (for faeries are discreet beings), then it is for you to decide. If you wish to hold the dedication in your home, which is usually the most convenient place, then you need to use your own faerie altar as a focus. The same applies if you are going to use your garden for the occasion. If you are to hold your dedication elsewhere, then you will need to take a portable altar with you. This may be something as simple as a small green cloth to cover a tree stump and a selection of the things that you usually have on your home altar. Candles are a must for your dedication, and the colour green would be the most appropriate for this occasion. Also make sure that you take a special gift for your Faerie King or Queen. You may like to burn some incense that will attract the faeries.

Prepare your altar for the dedication. You can decorate it with flowers, moss and night lights, faerie lights, swathes of muslin, scattered rose petals and lavender, in fact anything that inspires you to honour the faeries and makes you feel as if you are almost in a part of the faerie realm yourself. Put the answer phone on, make yourself look wonderful and prepare to enter the place of faerie magic.

As for your appearance, faeries will not be impressed by someone who doesn't try to look their best. Your body is an aspect of the divine, a sacred being, and during a ritual you should look your very best, even if the rite is worked alone, for you will meet the Faerie King and Queen, who honour all beauty and sacredness.

One word or warning: don't make your dedication a completely sombre affair, for faeries greatly dislike solemnity. You will find that things will not go quite according to plan if dignity and sobriety are what you have in mind. Faeries do like at least some element of silliness and chaos and they will always get their way. A candle may get knocked over, you will get the fit of the giggles, your cat might drink your gift of the finest cream to the Faerie Queen, you may set the fire alarm off with your incense smoke – you get my drift. So please don't make it pious or serious, or the wee folk will take a mischievous hand in the proceedings! Although of course this is a dedication with serious intent and life-changing consequences, nothing's ever *that* serious. If you don't add a bit of silliness yourself, the faeries will remind you to – and these are the faeries you are working with, remember. So add a verse or two that rhymes badly, wear some faerie wings and a tiara if it makes you feel better, put disco glitter in your hair, sing the whole dedication to the tune of *Dancing Queen* by Abba – what the hell! This is faerie magic, anything goes and nothing is set in stone. Freedom and creativity are the watchwords and real faerie magic stems from them. Laughter is the best spiritual energy that you can work with. In witchcraft there are two words which are always adhered to in ritual, and they are *reverence* and *mirth*. Be ever mindful of this combination in faeriecraft and you will have struck the perfect balance.

Here is a faerie dedication that might inspire your creativity:

Stand before your fey altar and place the gift to your Faerie King or Queen there. Tell them why you are here with a statement of intent:

'Dearest Faerie King and Queen,
my elfin mentors who are unseen,
to learn the magical faerie art
is the wish within my heart.'

Once you have presented your faerie gift and statement of intent, sit down before your altar and prepare yourself for meditation. Open your chakras, visualize your protection and work through your relaxation exercise. This meditation is the faeries' gift to you and will not follow the usual pattern of a pathworking. In this meditation you will make your own parameters and decide which pathways to take and when to come back. I will merely provide you with the invocation; you must make the journey. On your journey, expect a faerie gift and also take a travelling companion such as your Faerie King or Queen, as they will protect you throughout the journey.

'Dear Faerie King and Queen,
take me to the land of green,
to the realms where no one knows
of the land of elves and trows.
Faerie Land is not quite here,
through the arch in another sphere.

An enchanted place,
through time and space.
Take me away.
Be sure to bring me back today.
Blessed Be.'

This invocation was received in St Michael's Tower on Glastonbury Tor, 29 July 2004.

Now go on your pathworking journey.

When you have completed your dedication path-working and received your meditational faerie gift, open your eyes and come back to yourself. Close your chakras and work through your grounding exercise.

You may like to tell your Faerie King or Queen about your feelings upon becoming a Faerie Priest or Priestess. You may have a poem which you would like to read out or, if you are musical, a piece of music to play. This is the part of the dedication that is personal to you and should come straight from the heart.

Once you have imparted your feelings to the faeries, then finish the dedication with a concluding statement:

'I claim the faerie priesthood.
With you I follow, pixie-led,
to use this gift for only good.
A magical path to faerie tread.
Blessed Be.'

When you have completed the dedication, do remember to eat and drink something. If you have dedicated with friends, then make this party time. You are now one of the faerie priesthood and your journey along the faeriecraft pathway really begins right here.

After you have worked any kind of magic, making sure that you come back to reality is very important. Before you begin your feasting, extinguish any candles that you have used and if you are working indoors, switch on the electric lights. This brings you back down to earth with a bump and places you firmly in the everyday. Shift everything back to the mundane and concentrate on celebrating your faerie priesthood.

Where Is the Faerie Temptress Taking Us?

As already mentioned, I believe the faerie temptress is the origin of the faerie priesthood. She is our magical and historical link to our ancient and legendary past. She is also the emergence and the unfolding of the faerie priesthood in the new millennium, the luminary echo and blueprint for us to take inspiration from. She has taken us this far, now it's our turn to lead the way.

If you would like to experience the energy of the faerie temptress and tempter and perhaps receive messages from

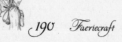

them, I have included two pathworkings for you to call upon them and perhaps take a leaf out of their book. Both the tempter and the temptress in these pathworkings were considered to have led a mortal life; however, both were also associated with the fey. Upon their death they were classified as part of the elfin realms and so qualify as a temptress and tempter. I have included both a male and female example so that you can follow the pathworking you are most drawn to. You may even wish to follow both of them at some time.

Faerie Enchanter: Robin Hood

At first you may think this an odd inclusion in a book on faeries, however Robin Hood is not quite the man the history books depict. Everyone knows the legend of Robin Hood and his band of merry men living in Sherwood Forest in Nottinghamshire and his romantic alliance with Maid Marion. Such is his magical renown that in some traditional witch covens the High Priest and High Priestess are referred to as Robin and Marion. Robin's magical connections do not stop there. Many sources link him with the woodland faerie Robin Goodfellow, who was mischievous and prankish and a friend of the ordinary people. Robin Hood may or may not have been Robin Goodfellow, with his clothes of green and his infamous arrows (both faerie traits). Upon his death, though, he certainly entered the magical realms of faerie, melding with such figures as Robin Goodfellow and Puck from Shakespeare's *A Midsummer Night's Dream*. Below is a pathworking to experience his realm and share a little of his magic.

Pathworking of the Enchanted Sherwood Forest

Prepare yourself for meditation in the usual way. If you can do this pathworking outside, all the better. If this is not possible then it does not matter, as your imagination will carry you there of course. Some time ago Neil and I visited Sherwood Forest and saw the enormous tree that Robin Hood is said to have hidden in. I have made the tree a central theme of the pathworking.

It is early autumn and the time is twilight. You are at the edge of Sherwood Forest and you can hear strains of merry music coming from deep within the wood. You begin to walk along a well-trodden pathway, following the sounds of the music and laughter. As you walk, newly fallen leaves scrunch underfoot. You carry a candle lantern on a stick before you and feel quite safe walking alone on such a beautiful evening. The air is warm and the forest feels like a merry, welcoming place.

As you walk farther into the forest, the music and laughter gradually become louder. You feel that very soon you will be among the revellers. There is a sense of excitement in the forest, and you too feel excited at the thought of what you will find. You notice the nocturnal animals and birds of the forest beginning to emerge as the evening draws in. An owl hoots softly from a tree as you pass, and you see hedgehogs scurrying noisily and busily through the pathway of leaves.

All of a sudden the music stops and so does the laughter, just as you thought you were about to come to the woodland party. Instead you turn a corner, and before you is an enchanting sight to behold. You have come across a forest clearing, but it is illuminated with what must be a hundred lanterns suspended from branches, tucked in nooks of trees and forming a circle in the magical glade. There is an air of mystery and enchantment, as if you have stumbled upon a faerie grotto. You also have the feeling that you are being watched, not in a sinister way but with curiosity and mischievousness.

In the centre of the forest glade is the most enormous tree that you have ever seen. It is an oak. Its girth is huge and there is a cavernous entrance in the trunk, large enough for several men to enter at once. This entrance is lit by lanterns hanging on branches that are stuck in the earth. Suspended around it are little bells that tinkle in the breeze, acorns threaded on string and wooden wind chimes clanking gently in the autumn wind. This entrancing sight seems to be a bewitching invitation to enter the tree.

You walk into the glade, illuminated by the lanterns, and all at once feel as if you have entered another realm, a magical place, not of this time or this Earth. As you walk into the tree, again you feel a shift in the atmosphere and now you are in a different realm entirely. The tree trunk is completely hollow and the woody walls are lit by torch flames. You feel safe in the tree, encircled and held by the earth and all its magic.

As you look around you, you see things that you feel could belong to Robin Hood in nooks and crannies in the tree trunk. In a knotty alcove lies a quiver of arrows, as if waiting to be used. Hanging from an inner branch is a green velveteen hat, almost moss-like, with a single feather in its side. In another woody nook is a goblet fashioned entirely from wood. You touch the goblet and it is exceptionally smooth, something only elfin hands could have created. On another wooden hook hangs a horse's bridle made from the finest and softest leather and trimmed in moss-green velvet. You feel honoured to be in Robin's realm and you feel that he could have just left the tree trunk hideout seconds before you arrived. You can almost touch his presence in the hideout, yet you instinctively feel that he and the rest of the forest revellers do not wish to be seen.

You leave the tree hideout and walk back into the glade. It is totally night now and the tree lanterns sparkle and wink in the moonlight, swaying in the breeze.

As you leave the woodland clearing you hear music and laughter once again. Their revelling had been suspended for you to enter at least part of the forest magic. As you walk along the pathway, back to where you first began your journey, you feel something in your pocket. You reach in and pull out the feather that had been in Robin Hood's moss-green cap. Taking this piece of magic home with you, finally you reach your destination, the edge of the forest.

When you are ready, open your eyes. Don't forget to close your chakras firmly, earth yourself and eat and drink something.

Blessed Be.

Faerie Enchantress: Vivienne

Vivienne is closely associated with Morgan Le Fay of Arthurian legend. She has many identities, enchantress being just one of them. She was believed to live a dual life, one as a faerie and the other as a charmed mortal. She is also known as Vivien, some know her as Niniane or Nimuë and of course she is universally referred to as the Lady of the Lake, who was believed to live in a crystal castle built by the magician Merlin beneath a lake. In this guise she bestowed on King Arthur the magical sword Excalibur, which was reputed to be a gift from Faerie Land to shield him from harm.

Legend also states that Vivienne took the knight Lancelot from his earthly mother when he was only a baby and raised him in the faerie ways in her underwater realm, preparing him for greatness in his adult life.

Pathworking of the Faerie Lake

Prepare yourself for meditation in the usual way. Vivienne is a vision and she will allow you to glimpse her for a short while.

Imagine that you are in a dense woodland. It is early spring, the time of beginnings and unfolding energy. You are out walking and it is starting to rain gently. The sun is still shining, though, and you expect to see a rainbow later on. As you carry on walking, you come across a large lake in the woodland. The water appears to be alive – as the rain plashes down, it bounces up again, causing bubbles and a great movement on the surface of the lake.

You stop in your tracks at the lake's side, knowing that you have been drawn there. For a while you feel mesmerized by the splashing and bubbling of the water. It is as if the rain is preparing the lake for a special happening, a magical meeting of the heavens and the underworld.

As you concentrate on the water, you notice the reflections in the lake are not those of the woodland. You see no reflections of trees or bushes, but instead a shimmering image of a lovely castle is beginning to take shape. This fortress is not of the woodland; it belongs to the lake in all its beauty.

The castle is a captivating sight and you are transfixed, in awe of its beauty and majesty. It is a crystal castle, glinting and gleaming in the rainbow sun's rays. Its walls seem so fine that they are almost transparent, although you cannot see beyond them.

For a fleeting moment you see someone coming out onto a balcony, as if looking up into the woodland. She seems to be surrounded by a sparkling white mist. Her long fair hair drapes over the walls of the balcony, plaited and studded with small white lilies. She has a very calm energy and brings peace to your whole being. She is an exceptionally beautiful creature with fine pale features and large limpid eyes. Her petite frame is covered in a white dress with silver braiding. Although delicate in appearance, she also emanates a powerful enigmatic presence. Vivienne is a being of great magical power and womanly guile. You see her drop some white petals over the castle balcony, as if she is sealing a wish. She then disappears as quickly as she came, vanishing behind the castle walls.

The reflection of the castle begins to flicker and slowly fade away, as if it were always an illusion. The rain gently slows, and beyond the lake you see the faintest of rainbows appear, almost as if that is an illusion too. You pick yourself up and at your feet see a scattering of white rose petals. You pick one up. You may make a wish with it and throw it into the lake. When you have done this, walk back into the dense woodland.

When you are ready, you may open your eyes and come back to yourself. Close down your chakras, ground yourself and eat and drink something.

Blessed Be.

The Faerie Temptress 197

The Faerie Priesthood

As you have probably gathered from this chapter, accepting the faerie priesthood is a lifelong commitment and definitely not a choice that everyone will want to make. If you do not feel drawn to taking on the priesthood, then the exercises in this book will still be totally valid for you. The faerie priesthood is not for everyone and is not a decision that you should take lightly. It may take months, or even years of soul-searching before you decide to take it on – it certainly did in my case.

If you do decide to follow the faerie pathway more closely and become a Faerie Priest or Priestess, don't expect your life to be any easier than anyone else's, but allowing your magical and faerie heritage to shine through your being will put you in touch with your deeper self and the wonderful Otherworlds of Elphame.

9

Wave Your Wand and Part the Cloud

The Tools and Attire of Faeriecraft

'She filled my every sense and made me feel as if I was
full of stars, full of the swirling universe in my very self.
She reached out her hand of light and blinked her enormous
elfin eyes and then I knew – I knew who she was. "Queen
Mab," I whispered and she smiled her entrancing smile and
burst before our eyes into a thousand beams of moonlight,
scattering around the circle of trees, filling our woodland circle
with her presence.'

ALICEN GEDDES-WARD,
'THE KISS OF TWO WORLDS'

Tools of Faerie Magic

The tools you need to perform a faerie ritual are very simple and certainly do not need to be expensive. These tools are magical implements and should not generally be used for any other purpose or by anyone else, unless it is an emergency or you specifically request it. Your faerie tools should be revered as sacred objects and treated as such.

Most of the tools that I mention in this chapter have their origins in wicca or in druidry. This is because there is a crossover between these magical systems and faeriecraft, and certain tools are used by all practitioners of magic. 'The tools, the physical objects we use in witchcraft, are the tangible representatives of unseen forces', explains the author Starhawk in *The Spiral Dance*. In faerie magic we utilize many of the same tools as wiccans, if sometimes with a little faerie modification or two!

The basic tools you will need for faerie magic are as follows:

- *A traditional broom*, or witch's besom, as it is known, made from an ash stake, with birch twigs and a willow binding. In faeriecraft they are decorated, so when you make or buy yours, tie it with ribbons, silver charms, lengths of threaded acorns, etc. and make it something really special. My own besom is adorned with silver threads and ribbons. I have sprayed it with glitter and inscribed

magical names and symbols onto the handle. It is my favourite working tool and I have had many magical and psychic experiences with it. I and my fellow covenors even saw blue sparks fly from it during one ritual. The besom has many uses in spellcraft and ritual, but its main purpose is to sweep your sacred space ready for the ritual. It will sweep away all everyday energies and negativity. This is your very first ritual act.

- *Two small bowls* which are used as containers for salt and water. My own are wooden, but they can be china, glass, bamboo or any natural material you are drawn to, except

metal. For ritual purposes, you will need sea salt and the purest water you can find. This can be water from a sacred or holy well, a running stream or bottled mineral water.

An incense thurible or censer. These are used to burn natural incense on charcoal disks. They are usually a small dish with a removable lid with air vents in it. Some have handles and some have chains so that you can carry them around your magic circle to purify, invoke or banish, whatever your intent, with your chosen incense. Thuribles can be purchased from New Age shops quite easily, along with foil-sealed packets of self-igniting charcoal tablets for burning incense on. Unfortunately they are almost universally made from metal, as they have to be able to withstand intense heat. Sometimes you can find them made from terracotta, or you could fill a clay pot with dry earth or sand and this will suffice.

A chalice is a vital faerie tool and one that symbolizes the element of water. Chalices are commonly made from metal, though it is possible to buy wooden ones and a specialist wood turner can even make one for you. A chalice made from wood or glass is the ideal in faeriecraft, however if this is impossible then pure metals such as copper, gold or silver, with their associations with the moon, would be appropriate.

- *A wand* is another fundamental tool. This is used to direct your own energy and symbolizes your magical will, which will flow through it. It represents the element of air in faeriecraft and, along with your besom, will be your most used tool.

Your Wand

A wand is usually made from wood, although some people prefer a crystal wand. Wooden wands resonate especially well with the faeriecraft pathway, as they emanate a natural and subtle flow of energy.

There are many trees associated with faeries, and several are recommended for wand making. The willow tree is one of these, as it is deeply associated with faerie magic, being a tree that grows at the entrance to the Underworld, on the banks of water. The willow is often associated with Morgan Le Fay, the Faerie Queens of the Underworld and the moon goddess because of its proximity to water and affinity with witches in general. All these connections make the willow a tree with magical profoundness and certainly a willow wand is a wonderful wand for a faerie seeker.

Hazel is another tree with fey associations and is traditionally used in wand making. My own faerie wand is made from hazel. The hazel tree is connected with fertility, wisdom and divination. It is considered to be a faerie dwelling. In Ireland it is known as *bile ratha*, which means that it is a tree of the rath, the faerie home.

It is always preferable to make your own magical tools and wands are no exception. When you make a magical tool, your own energy goes into it, ensuring its sacredness and individuality from the very beginning. It is also much more economical, of course. If you do wish to buy a wand, at least try to purchase it from the craftsperson that made it. They can usually tell you its origin. It is often possible to buy magical tools from their makers at pagan conferences or from the internet. The makers are usually magical practitioners themselves and have a passionate interest in their craft, so you will be assured of a tool made with love and intent.

If you do decide to make your own faerie wand, here's how. First of all, choose which wood you would like to fashion your wand from. This may be determined by access to particular trees, being instinctively drawn to a certain tree or a combination of both. Choose a magical time to collect your wand wood. This could be a full moon if you have chosen willow, for example, or for hazel the sabbat of Midsummer, which is the traditional time for magically cutting hazel. If this is not possible, a full moon is always a favourable time.

Once, on the night of a full moon, two friends and I were walking along a pathway near a woodland to the site of our ritual. We had just been discussing wands when a large stick fell from a branch high above us and landed at one of my friend's feet. She stopped still before the fallen stick and then laughed, picking it up. She waved it about a bit and then said that someone faerie must have heard us, as it was just as if the wand had been delivered to her. She took it home and from that day on it became her personal wand, as she felt that it had been a definite gift.

If you are searching for a wand, it is always best to use wood that has already fallen from a tree. The guideline is that it should measure from your elbow to the tips of your fingers. Of course, any wood that is too long can always be cut to the correct length. Always thank the tree for the wand and leave a gift of milk, honey, etc. at the base of the tree or in a secret nook for the faerie inhabitants.

If you are unable to find a fallen wand, then you will have to cut one from the tree, although you need to go about this in the correct manner. Take time to tune into the tree's energies and ask it very politely if you may cut a wand for your magical use. Do not assume that it will allow this. If you feel that the tree is unhappy about it, then you will have to find another. Always make sure that you wait for the tree's answer. Once you have found a tree which is happy with your intentions, then cut only what you need. Thank the tree and leave a faerie gift for the rath dwellers.

Once you have received your wooden wand you can set about fashioning it to your own tastes and requirements. Some people prefer simplicity in their ritual tools, and if you feel this way, it is perfectly acceptable to leave the stick exactly how you found it or cut it. Alternatively, you may like to carve the two ends of your wand and strip the bark. This will still leave you with a beautiful simple wand but one that looks more than just a stick. As with most creative decisions in faeriecraft, it is up to you.

If you prefer a more stylized wand, there are many approaches you can take. With a sharp knife and sandpaper, you can cut the wand into a spiral shape and smooth it down, adding a crystal at the tip and studding it with small crystals at the handle, for example, and perhaps painting it with symbols, faerie animals, trees, herbs, etc. You can also wind coloured ribbons along the length of the wand and add feathers and tiny shells. Making your own wand will be a spiritual venture in itself.

Crystal wands are less easy to make at home than wooden ones and will usually require specialist tools to fashion. It is possible to make a quartz wand using sandpaper, but this requires a lot of time and dedication. Even if you buy a ready-crafted crystal wand, however, you can still make it more individual by winding ribbons, silver thread or thin leather strips along it. When a spiral, in whatever material, is wound down the length of a wand, the magical potential is greatly enhanced. You also add your own personal vibrations to the wand by customizing it in this way.

Another material commonly used in wand making and suitable for the faeriecraft pathway is selenite. This is a semi-precious material and will not only make an extremely attractive wand but also one with a pure and high energy flow particularly suitable for connecting with the angelic realms and the healing arts. Again, a selenite wand can be purchased ready fashioned or you can buy a rough one, sand it down yourself and decorate it.

A note of interest is that if you require any magical tool, it is always worth mentioning it to your guardian angel or Faerie King or Queen. Tell them exactly what you need and the style you would like and also why. You can even write your request down on a small piece of paper, fold it up and place it on your faerie altar. If you ask, the universe will generally provide you with what you need to follow your spiritual pathway. You may not find the tools in the place or way you envisaged, but they will be provided all the same. So, if you do not have the funds to buy tools or the means to make them, ask for help and somehow or another these tools will be provided. I have found many of my own magical tools at ridiculously cheap prices or have had them given to me as gifts out of the blue. Even most of my robes and cloaks were kindly given to me when I least expected them.

Do not concern yourself with *how* these things will enter your life, because that's all in the magic. Just know that you will receive the things you need when the time is right. Even if you feel that you don't need to ask for tools to come to you, then you may like to ask for the *right* tools to be made known to you and for guidance in making the correct choice. Always trust in the faeries and angelic realms and they will help you out. If you are a Faerie Priest or Priestess of theirs, then feel able to be held by the universe; their path is your path and so will ultimately be one filled with light.

Once you have found your wand, as with all magical tools, it will need consecrating to purify it and make it appropriate for use in the place between the worlds, a place nearer to the gods, faeries and angels than our mundane world.

Consecrating Your Wand

For consecration of any magical tool, you need to have representations of all the four elements present on your faerie altar. These may be incense smoke for air, a candle for fire, a bowl of spring water for water and a pot of herbs for earth.

Consecrations are best enacted on a full moon. If this is impossible, then a waxing moon will suffice. Prepare your altar beforehand and prepare yourself to come before the Faerie King and Queen.

Stand before your fey altar and place a small gift to your Faerie King and Queen on it. Tell them why you are here with a statement of intent:

'Dearest Faerie King and Queen,
my elfin mentors who are unseen,
consecrate my wand today
in your special faerie way.'

Then sit down before your altar and prepare yourself. Open your chakras, visualize your protection and work through your relaxation exercise. You are now going to go one step further into ritual than you did with your faeriecraft dedication. You are going to create a simple magic circle, one that will provide focus and protection but will not be as elaborate as the circle in a formal ritual. This is all good practice for the rituals provided further on in the book.

In your own words call upon the assistance of your guardian angel. Ask them to help you manifest a magic circle and oversee your consecration work.

Now visualize a circle of sparkling white light all around yourself. This circle spins with humming energy deosil (clockwise) and is a formidable boundary which nothing harmful may cross. For a few moments concentrate on sending a vibrant white light around yourself. Imagine that it is spinning so fast that you can hear it whirring.

You are now going to ask the four elements to be present, to bring elemental power to your consecration and also to assist you in your work:

'East bears air, the wind soars.
South frees fire, the flame roars.
West springs water as it flows.
North cradles earth; a seed grows.
Of all the elements far and near,
witness, bless and be present here.
So mote it be.'

Now take up your wand in the hand in which you will always wield it and say:

'Blessed Be, faerie wand of mine.
Serve me well, instrument divine.
Through you flows my magical will.
Between the worlds, be with me still.
My ally in Elphame, be by my side,
as the Faerie King and Queen are my guide.'

Now wave your wand through the swirling incense smoke, all the time imagining that the power of that element is imbuing your wand, and say:

'Wand of power, wand of mine,
charge with air and the spark divine.
Blessed Be.'

Next pass your wand through the candle flame, also visualizing the power that element is conveying to your wand, and say:

'Wand of power, wand of mine,
charge with fire and the force divine.
Blessed Be.'

Now sprinkle your wand with the spring water. If you have a selenite wand, do this extremely sparingly — just one drop will do — as water attacks selenite and will corrode your wand! Say:

'Wand of power, wand of mine,
charge with water and the essence divine.
Blessed Be.'

Lastly, press your wand into the pot of earth, visualizing its dense energy transmitting to your wand, and say:

'Wand of power, wand of mine,
charge with earth and the magic divine.
Blessed Be.'

Press the wand against your heart, saying;

'I dedicate this wand
to my faerie way.

My principal tool
to invite the fey.
Blessed Be.'

Then, in your own words, ask for a simple blessing from your own Faerie King or Queen upon your wand, dedicating it to your faeriecraft pathway.

When you have done this, place your wand on the faerie altar and focus on visualization once again. Imagine the four elements departing from your circle of light and say:

'Blessed Be, elements four.
Air, fire, water, earth, you came.
Depart through the faerie door.
Proceed to your realms with faerie name.
So mote it be.'

This marks the end of your wand consecration rite. Close your eyes and visualize the circle of white whirring light around you dissolving into thin air. Thank your guardian angel and then close your chakras firmly. Don't forget to work through a grounding exercise and drink and eat afterwards.

This wand consecration can be reworded for consecrating and blessing any of your magical tools. Have a go at devising your own charges and invocations in poetic form. Don't worry if they rhyme badly or even farcically, as the fey love a giggle and won't mind a bit. So there's absolutely no excuse if you're terrible at poetry – if it makes you laugh then the energy in your faerie circle will be fantastic!

More Faerie Tools

Another tool usually made from wood, although I did make my own from wax once, is the pentacle. This is a slim wooden disc which represents the element of earth on your altar. On it is engraved, painted or drawn a pentagram, which is the faerie witch's symbol of universal unity, spirituality and protection. A pentagram is a five-pointed star, and each point is aligned with a particular element: water, fire, earth, air and ether or spirit.

The pentacle is for grounding energy and can also be used to serve the ritual cakes or to stand your chalice upon the altar. It can also be made from a chosen faerie wood and is easy to make yourself. Alternatively, pentacles can be bought from many wonderful craftspeople. Some pentacles are not only decorated with pentagrams but also adorned with beautiful paintings or images burnt into the wood with pyrography.

Other items you will require for your rituals are candles, candle holders and an altar cloth.

There are many other tools available for magical practitioners, but these are optional and you can obtain them as and when you need them.

One of these is a staff. This is the equivalent of the sword in witchcraft traditions. A staff as a magical tool is more common in druidic pathways. The reason it is optional in faeriecraft is that it has much the same functions as a faerie wand, just on a larger scale.

A magical staff is usually made from wood and is a long, thick stick about the height of its owner, maybe taller. Again the tree it has come from is important in terms of magical significance and the staff may be decorated, carved with spirals and symbols to the faerie seeker's own desires and taste. As with the wand, the staff is used to direct the Priest's or Priestess's will through the flow of the wood. Unlike the wand, it has an aura of magical eminence and status. Throughout legend we see powerful magicians portrayed with their staffs, such as Merlin and the fictional Gandalf in Tolkien's *Lord of the Rings*.

If you opt for a staff too, then it would be a complement to your wand and, because of its size, ideal for outdoor faerie circles. All the same guidelines apply for making or buying a staff as for the wand. However, if you do wish to buy one, bear in mind that they are a rarer magical tool than the wand and you may have to wait a little longer and search harder for the one you want.

As a general guideline, the faeriecraft pathway honours simplicity and beauty, so resist cluttering your altar with tools you rarely use. Magical tools are simply a physical focus for your magical will and faeriecraft follows nature's tides. It does not touch the realms of high magic so does not require the elaborate tools of a ritual magician. Keep it simple and you can't go wrong.

The Book of Elfin

This is a book kept by every faerie seeker to record their dreams, spells, meditations, rituals and recipes. It is also a magical diary. It should be handwritten and decorated with your own drawings or leaves, flowers, pictures from magazines, etc. Suitable colours for the cover are green, purple or silver. This book should be kept confidential, as a private record of your faerie pathway, and should only be shown to another faerie seeker.

Building the Crystal Castle

If you have completed the exercises in this book so far, you have already laid the foundations for ritual. You have created a faerie altar and meditated on the elements of air, fire, water and earth. You have learned how to follow a pathworking, create your own psychic protection and use poetry to reach out to the fey. These are all integral skills required for rituals. You only have a few more things to learn to fill in the gaps. You are now going to expand on the skills we have already covered in order to incorporate them into your own rituals.

The key component of every ritual is the creation of a magic circle. This is usually not physically drawn or marked on the ground, although it can be if you so choose, but a circle visualized as a circumference of light.

The purpose of a magic circle is twofold: 1) to protect the Priest and Priestess from any unfriendly or unwanted energies and 2) to provide a focus and psychic boundary for the magical energy that is used in the ritual.

Once you have cast a faerie circle, or ring, as it is known in faeriecraft, you step into the place between the worlds where many of the rules of physical reality vanish and you honour the ways of Faerie Land. Once a circle has been cast time has a will of its own and may not follow in a linear fashion. You may think you have worked a ritual for half an hour maybe, but when you close your chakras and look at your watch, it may have been three hours. This is not at all uncommon, in fact it can be a regular occurrence, as you are working with faerie time. This kind of time-warping is especially noticeable on sabbats such as Samhain and Beltaine, when the veil to Faerie Land is thin and mischief-making is abundant in the fey realms.

Every time you work a ritual a new ring is cast and at the end of the rite the circle is banished. A faerie circle is not a permanent structure for practical reasons. If you are working rituals in your home, it would be irresponsible to leave your faerie circle intact, as any others walking in and out of it might pick up psychic residue, which would not be conducive to a grounded everyday life.

Also, once cast, a circle is like an astral light shining out to the other worlds. This light attracts both light and dark elements in the Otherworld and although during a ritual of a finite period it is easy to protect your circle from unwanted influences, it is not possible to do this effectively on a permanent basis.

Another reason is that it is important to make definite distinctions between your magical and mundane life. It is healthy to have a flow between them, however when it comes to ritual the boundaries must be drawn most distinctly and this world and the Otherworld must not be allowed to leak into one another or experiences such as astral benders and psychic hangovers will occur. A Faerie Priest or Priestess must live life with their feet firmly in reality, otherwise the balance is upset. After all, we are physical beings and are not meant to lead astral lives as the faeries do.

Casting a circle is often likened to building a castle, a strong fortress of protection and also a substantial structure to contain the magical energy that you will use. In the case of faeriecraft, we visualize a faerie crystal castle that shines and sparkles with beautiful shimmering light. There is also another variation from the casting of the circle in traditional witchcraft. In the craft an athame, or ritual sword, is used to direct the energy to cast a circle. In a faerie circle, we never use metal tools, as they are literally poisonous to the fey people. Therefore you would use a wand made of wood or crystal to cast your circle.

A Crown of Raindrops

In the previous chapter I touched on what to wear for a ritual. Here are a few more pointers to get you ready for your faerie circle.

If you are a solitary Faerie Priest or Priestess, you will not have to observe a group consensus on dress and may have more freedom in what you wear. When considering what to choose as your magical garment, it may be helpful to think about what connects you to faerie. This might be something seemingly frivolous, but that does not matter, as the fey do have a playful side of course. When I put my ritual dress on, which is in a style reminiscent of mediaeval times, I do feel almost ready. However, the things that really connect me to faerie are my crown or tiara, my shoes and wand. All these finishing touches make me sparkle inside and it is only then that I feel prepared to work magic. This is all psychological of course, and I do not actually *need* these things to perform a ritual, but they make me feel very faerie indeed, as if I have just stepped into the Land of Elphame. And that's the key you need to find: something that makes you feel magical and out of this world. It may be something as simple as a necklace that you wear only for ritual or you may even have a pair of dressing-up faerie wings!

Another adornment which can help you enormously to link to faerie is a crown of some sort. This is simply because unless you are actually royalty you are highly unlikely to wear one of these in everyday life, therefore it will instantly be your key to Faerie Land. This may sound expensive, but does not have to be at all. You can go out and buy a crown or tiara from a shop. Some pagan and wiccan jewellers also make them in some very beautiful and individual

styles suitable for a faeriecraft ritual. However, these are likely to be fairly expensive and you need to consider your choice very carefully before purchasing.

The alternative is to make your own crown or tiara. This can be something as simple as a circlet of flowers if you are a Priestess or a circlet of leaves and berries if you are a Priest. These are very easily made, so straightforward in fact that if you have children they may like to help you make yours and you could make them a simpler version at the same time. My group and I once spent a whole afternoon on Beltaine making these and our children joined in too, which they thoroughly delighted in doing. The women and girls made circlets with hawthorn blossom and leaves and the men and boys made theirs from oak leaves.

All that you need to make a flower or leaf crown is some green plastic-covered wire (you can buy this from florists, garden centres or hardware shops), a pair of secateurs and a large bowl of cold water to keep your foliage fresh. Fashion the wire into a circle and wrap it around about three times so that you are able to stick stalks into the spaces in it. Make sure that you measure it on your head before you cut it to size. Once you have cut it, wind some tape or ribbon around the end you have cut so that it does not stick into your head. Before you attach your flowers or foliage, you may like to decorate your crown with trailing ribbons at the back, little bells on a thread, acorns and other small items stuck on and bendy twigs winding around the wire to create a more natural feel. Be inspired by your natural surroundings or whatever is available to you and go with the flow.

You will then need to collect flowers or foliage with decent length stalks. You can poke these into the gaps between the wire and if they are not secure enough, then also wrap the stalks with thread in a colour that will blend in. Just as a tip, don't leave gaps, as you don't want any unsightly wire showing. You can always wind ribbon in the gaps if you do not have enough flowers or leaves. Place your crown in a bowl of cold water until you are ready to wear it. It should float!

If you are making your circlet in spring or summer, then a more natural material to make the band out of is cleavers (goose grass), also sometimes known as 'sticky weed'. This grows abundantly in most British hedgerows and verges. Simply pick a good-sized handful that is long enough to make a circle around your head. When you get it home, lay it out on the table or floor. Avoid putting it on the carpet, as it will stick to it! Bunch the stalks and twist them together, then fashion them into a circle to fit your head. The ends will stick together naturally with a little twisting. If you are a Faerie Priest, you may like to leave your circlet plain or add some berries if they are in season. If you are a Faerie Priestess, you can add blossom or almost any type of flower, including roses. The stalks can be easily stuck into the twisted cleavers and will hold remarkably well without any other attachment. The result is a very natural-looking and lush flower crown, befitting of the season that you made it in. If you have made it a few hours in advance of your faerie circle, then place it in a bowl of cold water to keep it fresh, otherwise it will wilt very quickly and you will neither look nor feel very magical. Do be aware also that any natural crown will only last for one night. The best thing to do is to put it on your compost heap the following morning and give it back to the earth.

A natural tiara can also be made from scratch with bendable wood such as willow, which is pliable when wet. You can decorate your willow circlet with sparkly beads threaded on very thin copper wire and wound around the base. You can do the same with acorns, pine cones, other natural finds in the woods or seashells. This will be a headpiece that could last some time if stored carefully. Store it in a hatbox to keep it from getting dusty or damaged.

10

The Faerie Ring

Celebrations for Groups and Solitaries Working with Faerie Magic

' ...weave the words with me,
the words that will entwine,
to the place between the worlds,
betwixt the kiss of night and day.'

ALICEN GEDDES-WARD,
'THE KISS OF TWO WORLDS'

Rituals Are a Faerie Thing

This chapter gives you, the faerie seeker, a taste of magic with some simple celebrations in ritual form. Rituals are an expression of our need to mark significant events in our lives and there are many different ways to observe them. As already mentioned, faeries follow the tides and celebrations of the Old Religion, the eight sabbats of the wheel of the year. Being spiritual creatures of the Earth, they naturally follow the ebb and flow of the seasons' cycle and are really the connoisseurs of ritual and celebration. If you mark a sabbat with a ritual, you can be assured that the faeries will be doing the same, only their party will go on three times longer than yours. They are masters of ritual and revelling, a duo that go together like strawberries and cream.

When we enter a ritual, we enter a sacred place, a place between the worlds, a fragment of Faerie Land. A ritual is quality time, if you like, to spend with the faeries, for it is an intense focus on the inner worlds. Every ritual, being a magical act, brings about an inner unfolding within us. It can be space to regain a sense of perspective in an increasingly complicated world. It is also a space where we can experience non-physical beings and realities in a safe and benign environment. For me a ritual is a window of peace and sanity, a place to get back in touch with myself and to meet and celebrate with the angels and faeries. It is my place of inner empowerment. Rituals are times to be cherished.

A ritual can be purely celebratory or it can have a function: to send healing to a friend, to cast a spell for someone in need or to mark an important spiritual or life event. If you have never performed a ritual, do not be put off by the word. Every celebration in our culture is a type of ritual, be it a wedding, christening, funeral or eighteenth birthday party. The rituals in faeriecraft mark the turning of the seasons, and important events and are just elaborations of the faerie dedication which you have already made. In this chapter I will take you step by step through performing a ritual, either on your own or in a group.

Recipe for a Faerie Ritual

I call this a *recipe* because all rituals have a basic unwavering format, a bit like pathworkings. The reason a format is used is so that both you and the other realms know where you are. A ritual is a set procedure, a celebration framed around particular events. This does not mean that it cannot be creative, impulsive or spontaneous – it is just that you are able to place all the ingredients in a well-practised and safe framework.

I have included four rituals in this chapter, two for solitary faerie seekers and two for groups. Whether working in a group or alone, the format remains the same, the only difference being that when you work in a group, the tasks of the ritual are shared and some duties are determined by male and female roles, as in a wiccan ritual. However, when working alone, it is perfectly natural to take on all the tasks yourself.

Below is a recipe for a faerie circle. It includes explanatory notes for groups and solitaries.

Preparing to Be Magical

Before any ritual, always take a cleansing bath or shower, using herbs and or oils to aid you in the magical ritual ahead. Even if you have no appropriate herbs, a handful of sea salt will always act as a magical cleanser.

Dress in your robe or special ritual clothes and put on the jewellery that connects you with faerie and any other items that transport you to Faerie Land.

Some people prefer not to eat a meal or to only eat a light meal before a ritual. This is because food grounds us to the Earth plane and if you have a full stomach it is more difficult to reach the altered state of consciousness required to enter the Otherworlds. So if your ritual is in the evening, for example, your last proper meal will be at lunchtime and just a snack at your usual mealtime will suffice. You can eat a proper meal at the feast after your rite.

The Faerie Altar Is Prepared

The altar takes on the symbolism of the time at which the ritual is set. If you are working at full moon, for example, then you may want to use a white or silver altar cloth and altar candles in the same colours. You might place other items on your altar corresponding to this time, such as white objects and food, and you might burn a full moon incense recipe. If it is a ritual of one of the fey sabbats, then an altar cloth in a colour mirroring that season would be appropriate. For example, at Samhain an orange or black cloth would be a good choice to echo the typical celebrations of that season. However, if, to begin with, your funds only stretch to one altar cloth for all seasons, this is fine. Green would be the best choice for an all-purpose faerie altar cloth.

Prepare your altar to reflect the ritual you are working and never skimp on this. This is because your altar is your link to Faerie Land, the physical focus of the emotional and spiritual energy that you need to contact your Faerie King and Queen. Tend it well.

Open your Chakras

If working solitary, sit down in the middle of the floor in the centre of the space where you intend to create your ritual and open your chakras. Ask for protection and guidance as usual.

If working in a group or with a partner, sit down and hold hands with one another to create the first connection of the circle working together.

Sweeping the Faerie Circle

Take up your besom and beginning at the faerie altar, sweep the perimeters of the circle in a deosil (clockwise) direction. Actually touch the floor with the broom, as if you are sweeping real dust away. Really give the circle a firm and thorough sweeping, visualizing as you go all the everyday and negative energies being swept away. Sweep the circle once, ending where you began at the faerie altar.

The circle can be swept silently, but some faerie seekers like to use a 'sweeping rune'. You can devise your own or use the following:

'Sweep, sweep, stardust deep,
magic in my circle sleeps.
Sweep, sweep, open my eyes,
Elven circle, come alive.'

I have used this sweeping rune for
many years and it is a simple, effective
and easily remembered part of the rite.

Consecrating the Salt and Water

On your faerie altar you have two bowls, one contain-
ing spring water and the other sea salt. Both of these need
to be consecrated, so that you can then use them to purify
your circle.

Take up your wand and dip the end into the bowl of
water. Concentrate on bringing energy from the earth and
drawing it up through your chakras until it reaches your
solar plexus chakra. Imagine projecting this energy in the
form of pure luminescent violet light through to your hands
and down your wand, infusing the spring water with a violet
glow.

Water is an element which requires ritual cleansing
because it can easily contain contaminants either visibly or
indeed invisibly, such is its nature. For this reason we need
a water purification invocation:

'Banish all impurities, be now water clean,
by the name of the Faerie King and Queen.
Water of the sparkling spring,

cleansing qualities to us you bring.'

After you have purified your water, turn your attention to your bowl of salt. This is consecrated slightly differently from water, as salt in itself is a purifying substance and so cannot be cleansed as such.

Dip the tip of your wand into the bowl of salt and, as with the water, draw energy from the earth and project it out of your solar plexus, down your hands and wand and into the salt in the form of violet light. Say:

'I bless this salt. From sea you came,
in the Faerie King and Queen's name.
From my circle banish all ill,
with the aid of my magical will.'

Now tip three portions of salt into the bowl of spring water and stir it well. Take this saltwater mixture and walk deosil round the perimeter of the circle, starting at your altar, sprinkling it with the tip of your wand as you go. (If you have a selenite wand, do not do this with your wand, but use the tips of your fingers instead.) As you walk the perimeter, visualize your circle being purified and consecrated by the sprinkling saltwater.

When you reach the altar at the completion of your circle, also consecrate yourself by splashing a few drops of the water over your head and body. If you are working in a group, then the person who enacted the salt and water consecration will sprinkle everyone in the group with a little saltwater to consecrate them too.

At this point in the ritual, your incense thurible can be taken deosil around the perimeter of the circle, all the time visualizing the spiralling smoke purifying your sacred space.

Casting Your Faerie Circle

In witchcraft covens this particular part of the ritual would normally be performed with the aid of an athame. In faeriecraft you would use your wand.

Casting a faerie circle is a powerful act where you project a circle of light into the ether encompassing you. Visualization in the casting is all-important, as this is what will cement your circle and make it real and invincible.

Take up your wand once more from the altar and draw energy as you have done before up through your solar plexus and out of the wand tip. Your arms need to be directly level with your body, and you will feel a stronger surge of energy if you hold your wand with both hands.

Beginning at the north point before the altar, visualize violet light pouring out of the tip of your wand, creating a beautiful circumference of light. Build your crystal castle in your mind; visualize it surrounding your circle and protecting it. Walk slowly around the perimeter of the circle, and visualize a circle of light not only all around you but also enclosing you in a protective castle of violet light. Say:

'Dear Faerie Queen,
dissolve the dream.
Let this circle sing
by your Faerie King.

By my wand to seal,
make the circle real.
So mote it be.'

Once you have completed one circumference of the faerie circle, come back to your altar.

Invoking the Four Elements

When working a ritual, the Faerie Priest or Priestess always invites the four elements to be present. This is for many reasons. First, you are essentially working with natural forces, and to work in harmony with nature you cannot work without them: they are of course intrinsically linked. Also, working with the four elements enhances and empowers your magic and your entire ritual experience. In essence, by inviting the four elements to your ritual, you are also inviting the magic to be present.

To invoke the elements, you will need your wand once more. Begin by standing facing the east point, facing outwards. Hold your wand in both hands and raise them upwards, level with your body, pointing the wand towards the east point.

Once you have done this, visualize the element of air in any way you find easiest. If you are working in a group, then they can all assist in the task by visualizing the element with you. Imagine the breeze coming into your circle and empowering your rite. At a recent ritual on a still summer's night with my group in our woodland circle, I was enacting the invoking of the elements and at the moment that I said the invocation for air, a wind whipped up at the east point, then swept around the circle deosil, in huge gusts, rustling the leaves in the trees. Everyone in the group exchanged glances and burst into giggles of disbelief. Well, we did ask, I suppose!

Next, invoke the element with a few words. Use the same words each time, as that way you will be able to memorize them and concentrate on the visualization rather than reading from a book or piece of paper. Putting a little effort into memorizing will go a long way to enhance your magical experience. Here is my own faerie element invocation which I wrote in 1997 and have used ever since. You can use it as you work round your circle, stopping at each cardinal point to visualize and invoke the appropriate element: air in the east, fire in the south, water in the west and earth in the north:

'I call upon the Guardians of the East,
the sylphs of air.
We invite and invoke you,
by the whispering wind.
We call upon you to commune with us
and protect our rite.
So mote it be.

I call upon the Guardians of the South,
the salamanders of the flickering fire.
We enchant and invoke you,
by the summer's warmth.

We call upon you to commune with us
and protect our rite.
So mote it be.

I call upon the Guardians of the West,
the undines of the shimmering water.
We beseech and invoke you,
by the sparkling rain.
We call upon you to commune with us
and protect our rite.
So mote it be.

I call upon the Guardians of the North,
the gnomes of the fertile earth.
We call and invoke you,
by the seed sower and the moonrise,
by the earth that is her body.
We call upon you to commune with us
and protect our rite.
So mote it be.

Of all the elements far and near,
witness, bless and be present here.
Hail and welcome.'

Then place your wand back on the altar.

The Faerie Ring 233

Invoking the Faerie King and Queen

In a witchcraft coven, at this point they would invoke the God and Goddess. In a faerie circle, we invoke the Faerie King and Queen instead, inviting them to be present for the duration of the ritual and bringing their actual etheric presence within the faerie circle.

If you are working a solitary ritual, you will already have a Faerie King and Queen with whom you have nurtured a relationship during earlier meditations. However, if you are working in a group situation, you will need to arrive at a consensus for a group King and Queen agreeable to everyone. As with all magical work, the decision will usually be made a little easier for you, as you will find that faerie monarchs often choose their group and not the other way around.

The invoking of a Faerie King and Queen also differs in style from a conventional coven, as witches would normally use a purpose-written invocation or inspired speaking. In a faerie circle we use poetry, as it is the language form that tempts the faeries most from their realms. This can be chosen from a book or verse that you have written yourself.

If you are working solitary, then you will invoke both the Faerie King and Queen yourself. If you are working in a group, then it is customary for a Faerie Priestess to invoke the Faerie King and a Faerie Priest to invoke the Faerie Queen into the circle.

To do this you need to stand before your altar, either with your palms turned outwards at either side of your body or raised, however you feel comfortable. In your mind, visualize the monarch you are invoking. You need to be very relaxed for invocation and in a meditative state, so take your time with this part and just let it flow.

Once you have a clear visualization of the Faerie King or Queen, then you can say your invoking poem. Once again, this will have a far greater effect if you can memorize it. Your poetry is your invitation to your faerie monarch to enter your circle and add their energy to your ritual work. It asks them to descend within you and literally infuse you with some of their power. It is said as a 'charge', which means that it carries direct energy to you. It should be said with feeling and intention, as you are of course asking for a magical act to occur and this always requires mental resolve.

If you are working in a group, then the partners performing the invoking would stand opposite each another before the faerie altar. The Priest would request that the Faerie Queen descend within his Priestess and the Priestess would request that the Faerie King descend within her Priest. Those invoking the Faerie King and Queen in a group are usually the leaders and for the duration of the circle are seen as embodiments of the faerie monarchs and should be treated with due respect.

Here are two poems which you may like to use when invoking the Faerie King and Queen, although of course you may like to write your own:

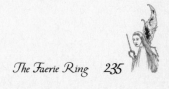

Invocation to the Faerie Queen

Faerie Priest: 'Come follow, follow me
your fairy elves that be;
And circle round this green,
Come follow me, your Queen.
Hand in hand let's dance a round.
For this place is fairy ground.
Queen Mab, intoxicating faerie of light,
Come with us on this full moon night.'

Anonymous English poem, seventeenth century

Invocation to the Faerie King

Faerie Priestess: 'His belt was made of mirtle leaves
Pleyted is small curious theaves
Besett with amber cowslip studdes
In which his bugle horne was hunge
Made of the Babling Echoes tungue
Which sett unto his moone-burnt lippes
Hee windes, and then his fayries skippes.
King Oberon, merry faerie of mirth,
Come with us on this rituals birth.'

Simon Steward, Oberon's Apparell, *1635*

While reciting your poem, you should at the very least
feel the presence of the Faerie King or Queen, so allow
yourself some time afterwards with your eyes closed to
become accustomed to their special energy. Previous work

with the King and Queen meditations should have prepared you for the type of feeling to expect, but invoking a deity can often be a very powerful experience. If you find that the energy they come with is too overwhelming, then you must tell them and ask them respectfully to dilute their energy for a while for you. After working with them over a period of time, you will gradually become accustomed to the full strength of their presence.

Do not rush this part of the ritual, as it is your connection with the divine and is an active and profound meditation. If you are working in a group, there is no need to feel self-conscious about a long period of meditative silence at this point. If you and a partner are invoking the King and Queen, then the rest of the group can join in the experience by sending positive energy to you and visualizing the monarchs descending into you.

The Raising of the Power

The 'power', or magical energy used to fuel 'the work' of a ritual, can be raised in many ways. In faerie magic we are seeking to enter Faerie Land, and so often the energy is sought by dancing or treading a spiral. We also use a chant to concentrate our minds and transport us into a deeper state of consciousness.

To raise the power in a group by dancing the spiral dance, everyone needs to stand in a circle and hold hands. The group begins by walking slowly and softly deosil, all the time visualizing a spiral of light beginning to grow in the centre of the circle. Gradually everyone begins to walk more quickly, eventually skipping and/or running, chanting louder and faster and reaching a climax. At this climactic point, everyone raises their arms above their heads, still with their hands clasped together, and 'rides the power', as I like to call it. This simply means that the whole group basks in the power they have raised. Raising the power can produce blissful states and feelings of oneness with the universe.

Another method which lends itself very well to faerie magic is what I call 'treading the spiral'. This produces very different and profound results. When working in a group everyone stands in a circle once again, however, with this method we do not hold hands. Each member of the group turns inwards to face their neighbour to the left, who will in turn be facing their neighbour, etc. The group then begins to walk slowly and deliberately deosil, all the time imagining that they are following a pathway which leads to Faerie Land. While treading the pathway, the group chants together, although this time it is in a whisper to create a trance-like atmosphere. With this method the pace of the walking or chanting does not quicken and instead remains constant, to allow concentration. Instead of reaching an exciting climax, the energy becomes dense and soporific and you will actually feel as if you are entering a different mind place. Once these changes occur, it is time for the group to hold hands, this time 'soaking in the power', rather than riding upon it.

If you are a solitary faerie seeker, the latter method will be more suitable, as you may not always feel like dancing all by yourself!

When choosing a chant for raising the power, once again poetry is the best means of connecting with the faeries. It is essential that this is completely memorized, as you cannot concentrate on visualization or attempt to dance and hold hands with a piece of paper in your hands! Choose something easy to memorize or an extract that rhymes well, which will always make things flow. Below is an example of a chant that I always use in faerie rituals. It is an extract from an old poem which never fails to carry us magically to Elphame:

> 'Round and round the faerie tree,
> Round and round dance we.'

This extract is taken from a longer poem. If you would like to look it up and use more of it as a chant, it is from 'The Terrible Head' by Andrew Lang, 1844–1912.

The Work

This part of the ritual focuses on the intention of your rite. Sometimes the time of year may shape the work that you do in your circle; a sabbat or a full moon, for example, will be the main theme. As well as any celebrations you can also include meditation, spellcraft, scrying, divination, trance work, healing, in short anything that you or your friends and family have need of. This is the time to bring it to the Faerie King and Queen in ritual.

If you work solitary, then this part of the ritual is your own creative choice and you are free to express it in any way you feel comfortable with or magically inspired by.

When working in a group, however, there will usually be a consensus on the theme of the ritual, and some or all of 'the work' may be planned beforehand. In magical work, especially, the group to which you belong is only as powerful as every individual that makes up the whole. For this reason, when part of a group ritual, individual faerie seekers are encouraged to take an active role. A ritual is not for spectators, and participants are expected to contribute to creating the energy required for magical experiences.

In summary, 'the work' is the main body of the ritual, the spiritual thread of the occasion. If you are solitary, it will be a total experience and if you are in a group, it will be a shared total experience. Neither is inferior to the other. In this part of the ritual you will have entered the doors of Faerie Land and you will truly be between the worlds.

Cakes and Mead

This is the time in the ritual when you show your appreciation to the fey by partaking in food and drink, traditionally cakes and mead (honey wine). After you have done this, always leave a small portion for the faeries, either on your indoor faerie altar or outside on a garden altar.

This part of the ritual is also a sacred rite as the Faerie King and Queen are imbued within the food and wine. To partake of this ritual offering is to consume a piece of magic, a gift from the faerie monarchs to us.

Before the cakes and mead are consumed, a blessing is said over them. This can often be something spontaneous and creatively inspired by the ritual's events, or it can be a suitable poem or extract from a poem. You could also use a piece specially written for your faerie rituals. There is an example below which you may like to use. If you are solitary, then take the plate of cakes and chalice and hold them up while saying your blessing. If you are in a group ritual, then the Faerie Priest and Priestess who have led the circle will take an item each and hold them up, saying the charge together.

Blessing for Cakes and Mead

'Blessed Faerie King and Queen,
I have trod your land of dream.
Now I seek to honour thee
with Elphame food that blessed be.
With this mead and honey cake,
of faerie food I do partake,
Two worlds are one within this rite
on this a most enchanted night.
Blessed Be.'

The cakes and wine are then sent around the circle with a kiss and 'Blessed Be' for the person next to you in the circle on your left. If you are in a group, the chalice will keep going round all the members of the circle until it is dry.

It is always best if you have made the cakes yourself or, in a group ritual, they have been made by the member most gifted at baking! The making of the cakes is a magical act in itself and another focus to prepare you for the ritual.

Ritual cakes are traditionally of an oat and honey based recipe. I use a recipe for ordinary flapjacks and substitute honey for the golden syrup. You can also add a few drops of wine to the mixture to make it a little more special and decorate the cakes with white icing if it is a full moon and silver confectioner's sugar glitter. Be creative: this is faerie food and a very special part of the ritual.

Of course there will be some times when you just cannot find the time to make cakes specially for a ritual. Whenever this happens I buy ordinary flapjacks from the supermarket. If you keep a pot of sugar glitter in your cupboard, all you need is a quick sprinkle and they are transformed for your ritual! Edible glitter can be brought from shops that specialize in cake decorating and one small pot will probably last you a couple of years, as a little goes a long way.

As for the mead, making it is a lengthy process requiring a lot of care. It is cultivated by the dedicated few. If you would like to try making it, I am sure you will be richly rewarded. However, selected supermarkets and wine merchants do sell it, though it is not as readily available as wine. If you really cannot find mead to have in your rituals, then red or white wine will suffice. Fruit juice, especially apple juice, is also suitable if you do not take alcoholic drink.

Farewell to the Faerie King and Queen

At the end of the ritual, it is imperative to send the Faerie King and Queen back to the realms where they belong. Whenever you invoke a deity in a ritual, they must always return whence they came.

Sending the King and Queen on their way back home is enacted in a similar way to invoking them. Stand before the altar as before and recite a few words, only this time visualize the King and Queen leaving your circle and disappearing into the ether. If you are working solitary, you would of course do this all by yourself. If in a group situation, the Faerie Priest would say farewell to the Faerie Queen and the Faerie Priestess to the Faerie King. Some poetry would be suitable, or these verses which I have written:

Farewell, Faerie King and Queen

Faerie Priestess: 'King of the Faeries,
blessed was your presence in this rite.
May you now return to Elphame
until we meet again.
Blessed Be.'

Faerie Priest: 'Queen of the Faeries,
blessed was your presence in this rite.
May you now return to Elphame,
until we meet again.
Blessed Be.'

Banishing the Elemental Quarters

This is done in the same way as invoking or 'calling' the quarters, except that this time you are reversing the intent. Take your wand from the altar and stand before the east point. Raise your wand in both hands so that it is vertical with your body and visualize that element departing from your circle. Do the same at each quarter. Here are some suggested words for banishing the elements:

'*Guardians of the East, sylphs of air,*
we give blessings for your presence here today.
May you now return to your realms.
Blessed Be.

Guardians of the South, salamanders of fire,
we give blessings for your presence here today.
May you now return to your realms.
Blessed Be.

Guardians of the West, undines of the water,
we give blessings for your presence here today.
May you now return to your realms.
Blessed Be.

Guardians of the North, gnomes of the earth,
we give blessings for your presence here today.
May you now return to your realms.
Blessed Be.'

Closing Your Chakras

If working solitary, then now is the time to sit down in the centre of your circle and firmly close your chakras. If in a group, then everyone would sit in a circle and, holding hands, close their chakras together.

Don't forget to perform a grounding exercise too. This is especially important after a ritual.

If working in a group, it is also customary to kiss everyone you have shared faerie time with, say 'Blessed Be' and have a friendly hug.

The Rite Is Ended

Once the ritual is completely over, if you are working indoors, then the electric lights should be switched on to bring you back to reality. This may seem a bit harsh, and it is a shame to extinguish the ambience of a candlelit room, but bringing you back with a bump helps with grounding.

The feasting can now begin and don't skimp on this bit, as it's all part of faeriecraft and is essential for grounding.

Faeriecraft Ritual Recipe

Here's a summary of the ritual structure. After a while you will automatically know the procedure and will not have to refer to this book.

Prepare yourself to be magical: bathe and dress
Prepare the faerie altar
Open your chakras

Sweep the faerie circle

Consecrate the salt and water: purify the circle,
    yourself and others

Purify your faerie circle with incense

Cast your faerie circle with your wand

Invoke the four elements with your wand

Invoke the Faerie King and Queen

Raise the power

The work

Cakes and mead

Farewell to the Faerie King and Queen

Banish the elemental quarters with your wand

Close your chakras: enact a grounding exercise

The feast begins!

Here is a summary of what you need on your faerie altar and the tools required for a ritual:

Altar cloth

Besom

Wand

Staff (optional)

Pentacle

Incense thurible or bowl

Charcoal discs

Natural incense and matches

Chalice

Candles and candle holders

Cakes

Mead

The Solitary Faerie Seeker

Many people prefer to work on their own as it gives total creative freedom. Working in this way you can celebrate the faeriecraft pathway exactly how you wish and when you wish. Working solitary brings an incredible sense of achievement and empowerment. Some people are solitary because they have to be, because of a shortage of local groups, and others are solitary because they would rather not work in a group, for whatever reason. Both ways of working have their strengths and weaknesses, but as long as you are aware of them, you can make your choice work for you.

Working solitary can mean that you are not held back by anyone else's pathway. You are your own spiritual boss and can set your own pace. The pitfalls are that you have to be very self-motivated to actually perform your own rituals. It is very easy to sit and watch television or go out with your friends instead of organizing a ritual. It is also very easy to cut corners and not do all the things that make up a safe and enjoyable ritual. Of course you will not be letting anyone down but yourself, but cutting corners can get you into deep psychic trouble if you are not careful. If there's no one there to remind you to close your chakras, then after a while you could get into the habit of leaving them open and there your problems may begin. So you can see why it takes a particular kind of person to work successfully as a solitary. That is why some people join groups, so that some of the self-motivation is taken away from them: the date of the ritual is in the diary, it is organized for them and all they have to do is turn up. However, if you cut corners or don't turn up in a group situation, then you not only let yourself down of course, but everyone in the group too. Faerie magic, of whatever form, requires responsibility and whether you choose to work solitary or in a group you remain a dedicant to the faerie King and Queen, which is a very special and responsible role.

I have worked both in a group and as a solitary at different times in my life. I now prefer to work alone with faerie or sometimes with my children and Neil. However, having been the founder and leader of a coven for many years, I still enjoy strong ties with that group and celebrate three or four rituals a year with them. I feel that I am in a very privileged position to be able to combine the two ways of working and to have a group that will allow me to visit as a guest priestess.

Even if you prefer working solitary, do try to seek out at least one person who can act as your spiritual mentor. This should be a special person who knows and understands your faerie pathway, someone you can turn to if you face any stumbling blocks. I have found working solitary extremely fulfilling, but I have only felt absolutely confident in doing so after working in a group where I had the guidance and support of others. You will hopefully find the best way for you at the right time in your life.

When performing rituals, as already mentioned, it is always best to work without a book or piece of paper in your hands. Therefore it is always good to use a pre-written ritual as inspiration for your own work. I have written two rituals for the solitary seeker. Here are 'Full Moon' and 'Faerie Treedom', which I hope will inspire you to create rituals of your own.

When presenting a ritual, I will not describe every detail in the 'ritual recipe' given earlier, but will describe 'the work' only, unless there are any changes in the preparation peculiar to that particular ritual.

Full Moon

As the title suggests, this ritual must take place on the night of a full moon, the faeries' favourite time for celebration and magic. For this ritual you will need three silver candles.

> Once you have raised the power in whatever way you choose, come and kneel before your faerie altar. This is the place of the Faerie Queen and the night of the full moon, a time of feminine energy, the optimum window to connect with her.

'Faerie Queen, secret and divine,
the enchanted orb draws me to your lights.
I wish to share the moon's delights,
catching moonbeams to be mine.

In between time and space,
beguiling and bewitching place,
moon shafts descend to me,
in this faerie circle be.

Faerie Queen, take my hand,
transport me to Faerie Land,
where moonbeams hang just like snow.
This silvery light I wish to know.'

Now light the three silver candles on your altar, slowly and deliberately, all the while visualizing moonbeams sparkling around the candle flames. By lighting your silver candles, you have symbolically invited in the moon and the energy of the moon goddess to your circle.

Once you have lit your candles, sit before your altar and close your eyes. You are now going to follow the 'moonbeam visualization'.

See the moon in your mind's eye in a bright starry sky with wispy silvered clouds, infused with the lunar sparkling glow. Concentrate on that image for a while and really breathe in the energy of the moon at its fullest. Tonight is the night of greatest magical power, the culmination of the moon's tide. Once the presence of the moon has taken hold of all your senses and nothing else seems to exist, you may capture moonbeams.

Imagine a beautiful shaft of silvery light gliding down from the moon right into your faerie circle. Visualize exquisite orbs of silvery light filling your circle with their celestial presence.

Once you feel that your circle is infused with moonbeams, imagine that they are circling around you, swirling in luminescent spirals of light.

Now take in a deep inward breath, and as you do so, visualize the moonbeams entering your being on that breath. Continue to inhale and exhale deeply and slowly, and with each breath, imagine that you are inhaling beautiful moonbeams and exhaling them again into the circle.

As you are breathing moonlight in and out of your body, you are slowly being filled with lunar light. Visualize the light spreading from the centre of your body and as you continue to breathe rhythmically, see the moonbeams spreading throughout your limbs, right down to your fingers and toes, and lastly filling your head.

When you feel that your entire body is filled with moonbeams, start to breathe normally again. Concentrate on your moon-filled body; see it in your imagination. You are now a being of light, at one with the heavens and the constellations. Take a while to discover what a moon-filled body feels like. You may feel a little dizzy, ecstatic, blissful even. Discover how it feels to be filled with the moon.

Faeries that belong to the moonlight will be around you now, dancing in your circle and floating on the shafts of light that descend from the silvery orb. Take in the experience and drink in this sacred time.

Once you feel that you have spent your time with the moon, then begin to breathe deeply once again. Imagine that with every in-breath you take in normal air and with every out-breath you exhale the moonbeams. Continue to do this until you feel that your body is clear of moonlight. If you have any problems eliminating all the light, then ask for the assistance of the Faerie Queen and she will help you.

Now visualize the moonbeams in your circle floating back up to the moon in a shaft of silvery light. Continue until your circle is back to the way it was at the beginning.

Once you have accomplished this, see the full moon again in the night sky and thank her for her moonbeam presence.

Once you have completed 'the work' of your ritual, then partake of your cakes and mead and close your ritual down, including closing your chakras and performing your grounding exercise.

Finish, of course, with your feast. On a full moon it is sometimes nice to feast with white food in honour of the moon's fullness. This is optional, but ideas are meringues, white bread, cream, nuts, cakes with white icing and sour cream and hummus dips. I have tried cakes with white icing and then silver sugar decorations. These are a nice moon-imbued touch.

Last of all, remember to leave an offering from your feast on your altar or in your garden for the faeries.

Faerie Treedom

This ritual can take place at any phase of the moon, however a waning moon would be ideal as this is a rite to explore your deeper self. On your altar, as well as your usual candles, you could have a brown or black candle to symbolize the earth. It is a rite to connect with the gnomes, so you may also like to place something on your altar to symbolize trees: acorns, candles, leaves, etc.

Prepare yourself, your altar and your circle for the ritual. The method of raising the power most suitable for this rite is 'treading the spiral'. Sit before your altar in a comfortable position and say an invocation to the gnomes:

'To the gnomes I invite your King
into the circle, please come in.
To follow a path I go seldom,
To tread the dream of faerie treedom.'

Now visualize the King of the Gnomes descending into your circle. He wears garments of brown and green and a crown of acorns. He carries a staff of twisted oak and comes with the energy of benevolence and the wisdom of the earth. He has a long grey beard which tapers down to his waist. Once you have visualized him entering the circle, then welcome him:

'Welcome to my circle divine,
a place of light, cast by thine.
Wise King of the Gnome,
take me to your home,
right through the oaken door,
to the place that you do adore.
Blessed Be.'

Now visualize the Gnome King placing a crown or tiara of acorns and leaves upon your head, a symbolic key for you to enter the realms of the gnomes. Now the King of the Gnomes will take you on a journey.

Imagine a majestic oak tree in the centre of your circle. In the trunk of the tree is a small wooden door,

carved beautifully into the oak. The Gnome King opens
the door and enters, and you follow him.

As you close the door behind you, you feel that you
are in the safest place you have ever been. The walls
are rooty and meet the earthen floor, which is a rich
red colour. There are torches flaming in the brackets on
the walls, producing a warm orange glow throughout
the inner tree trunk. You feel totally secure and held by
the earth.

The Gnome King has started to walk down an
earthy tunnel, rather like a large rabbit warren. He beck-
ons you and you too start to make your way down the
pathway. It is lit by torches and as you walk down it you
spy glinting amethyst and rose quartz crystals bejewel-
ling the walls. Everywhere is warmth and beauty.

The tunnel twists and turns, weaving and wending its way down on a slight incline all the way. At last the Gnome King reaches a jewel-studded door, glittering and shining with rubies and garnets. He opens the beautiful door and walks into a crystal chamber. It is glimmering with crystal pools of water and waterfalls running gently over sparkling semi-precious stones. There are also crystal caves within the chamber, with clusters of gnomes within them.

The Gnome King gestures for you to enter one of the beautiful caves. The gnomes within the cave part as you enter to reveal a stunning altar, fashioned by the roots and leaves of the oak tree. It is an obvious faerie altar with a chalice, crystal wand, plate of cakes, pentacle, thurible smoking sweet-smelling incense and brown candles with flickering flames. You instinctively reach into your pocket and find a stone in your hand. As you bring it out you see that it is a stunning uncut ruby. You know that you must leave it on the altar as a gift to the gnomes.

Also on the altar is a gift for you. It is a piece of parchment with a painting of a gnome on the front. You pick it up and turn it over. On the other side is a message written flamboyantly in deep brown ink. It is a message for you and you alone are able to read it. It is a personal message from the gnomes to help you in some way. You may stay there and ponder on your message as long as you like.

Once you are ready to leave the crystal cave, the Gnome King goes through the jewel-studded door and leads you through the wending, winding earthy passage-way once more. Soon you reach the oak tree entrance hall and the Gnome King indicates that you should leave through the wooden doorway.

You close the door behind you and visualize yourself back before your circle faerie altar once more. Visualize the oak tree in the middle of your circle dissolving and disappearing into thin air. Now complete your faerie freedom experience by thanking the Gnome King:

'Wise King of the Gnome,
I came to your home,
I went through the oaken door,
to the place we do adore.
Now I bless and honour thee,
revere the earth and Blessed Be.'

When you feel ready, you can open your eyes. If you are in need of a spell, now would be a good time for spellcraft and if your rite is taking place on a waning moon, a banishing spell would be appropriate.

Once you have completed the work of your rite, then bless your cakes and mead and close down your circle, eventually ending up with your feast and not forgetting to leave an offering from it on your faerie altar or in your garden.

The Enchanted Faerie Ring

Working in a group differs greatly from working as a solitary faerie seeker. I have termed a faeriecraft magical group a *faerie ring* and members of such a group *faerie seekers*.

Unlike witchcraft, the faerie pathway does not have an upper limit on numbers in a magical group and groups can consist of anything from three people to however many faerie seekers are comfortable working together.

If you would like to start a faerie ring, then be prepared for magical happenings. People who are drawn to the faeries will find one another, and magic is in their meeting. If you wish to work with the faeries in a group, then just ask them for some help and advice, but don't forget to listen and look out for their answers too. Be prepared for surprises!

To work in a faerie ring, it is also advisable to have a structure, as the faeries do in their society. The hierarchy is determined according to who founded the faerie ring or who has the most experience. There is no room for big egos in faerie magic, and it is helpful for everyone to remember that you are all learning together and every ritual is a growing and inner unfolding for all the faerie ring.

Within a ring, particular roles are taken on by individual members. The ring has one or two focal seekers, who are usually the founder or founders. These are *the Priest of Elphame* if they are male or *the Priestess of Elphame* if they are female. Both of these have helpers who assist them in the running of the ring and leading of the rituals. In my group we call these helpers *the King and Queen of Cobwebs*. They also perform the role of looking after newcomers to the group. During a ritual they always have the task of sweeping the faerie circle, hence their name.

Everyone else in the group is of course a Faerie Priest or Priestess in their own right and takes on other roles in the ring, such as treasurer, scribe, etc. As with any other club or society, a faerie ring needs to be organized to run smoothly.

The roles need not be set in stone, for all the ring's rites and seekers can swap roles if desired, so that everyone gains experience in all aspects of ritual.

The Priest and Priestess of Elphame normally perform most of the casting of the circle with the help of their King and Queen of Cobwebs. Before the ritual begins the King and Queen of Cobwebs will set up and prepare the altar. They also take on the task of looking after supplies for rituals, making sure that the members of the faerie ring have everything they need, such as cakes, mead, salt and candles, etc.

A faerie ring can also be single-sexed, and all-female and all-male groups can work equally well as a mixed-sex group. It's all down to personal preference. In a single-sexed group you would just have to arrange the roles of the seekers accordingly.

Working in a faerie ring can be an extremely enjoyable experience and members can become very close to one another by working rituals together. However, belonging to a magical group is always a learning experience and it is as much about the right combination of personalities as beautifully crafted rituals.

Here are two rituals written specifically for group working. One of them is an example of a sabbat rite.

The Beltaine Spiral

This ritual will of course take place on or close to the sabbat of Beltaine, 30 April/1 May. This is one of the Greater Sabbats and one of the most significant in the fey seasonal calendar. Along with Samhain, Beltaine is a time when the veil between the worlds is thin and movement from one world to another is favourable.

For this ritual you will need 2 yellow candles, approximately 16 yards/5 metres of green ribbon, 2 hawthorn flower crowns and a chalice of fruity wine, preferably strawberry, with rose petals floating on the top.

Once the altar and ritual room or outside space have been prepared, the whole of the faerie ring stands in a circle and holds hands. The Priest and Priestess of Elphame ask everyone to forget the world outside and focus on the time of Beltaine.

Everyone is quiet for a few moments and then, starting with the Priest or Priestess of Elphame, everyone present kisses the person on their left in turn, so that a kiss is sent deosil around the circle, and says 'Blessed Be.' Everyone then sits down and opens their chakras.

The King or Queen of Cobwebs then takes up the faerie besom and sweeps the circle, singing the sweep-

ing rune as many times as is necessary to complete the circle. The Priest and Priestess of Elphame proceed to consecrate and cast the circle and call the four elements before taking on the focal role of invoking the Faerie King and Queen. If, for whatever reason, the Priest and Priestess should be absent from a ritual at any time, then their deputies, the King and Queen of Cobwebs, can perform this.

Raising the power is then led by either the Priest or Priestess of Elphame. Dancing the spiral dance is particularly suitable for the energy of Beltaine. Once the power has been raised, then you can begin 'the work'.

As this is Beltaine, the night of faerie mischief, the Priestess of Elphame now chooses a male seeker from the ring to be 'Puck' for the evening. He now has licence to cause as much mayhem as possible whenever he likes. Previous Pucks on Beltaine night have chased everyone around the circle with the faerie besom, made people jump by creeping up on them, given people forfeits and announced silly games at a moment's notice! Puck is of course the prankish English faerie who dwells in the woods, and spring and summer are his time.

The Priest and Priestess of Elphame now choose one male and one female seeker from the ring to be the May King and Queen for the night. These are crowned by the Priestess of Elphame with the hawthorn circlets. Two faerie seekers from the group are then given one end of the green ribbon each. They circle around the May King and Queen in opposite directions and, as they do so, bind the couple together with the ribbon. The rest of the ring can dance around the couple at this point or stand clapping or chanting, whatever feels comfortable. This part of the rite invariably ends up with a lot of giggling, silliness and eventual chaos, and so it should, for that is the spirit of Beltaine, and the sillier the better, as it raises the energy and takes us to the Otherworld on this one special night.

Once the ribbons have come to their end, the May King and Queen are offered a sip each of the strawberry wine. This can also produce giggling and silliness as of course the May King and Queen cannot hold the chalice themselves, as they are bound by ribbons! Once they have managed to partake of the wine, they kiss once, symbolically sparking the beginning of this fertility Sabbat.

Priestess of Elphame: 'The sacred marriage has now begun,
For faerie magic, ribbon be unspun.'

This is the signal for the two faerie seekers to unbind the May King and Queen, circling widdershins this time.

The King and Queen of Cobwebs now take up the faerie besom and lay it north to south within the circle. They place the two yellow candles at either end of the besom, light one each and stand at either end of the besom to officiate over this part of the rite.

Queen of Cobwebs: 'Lit is the spirit of Beltaine.'
King of Cobwebs: 'Now jump the besom to enter the Land of Elphame.'

Everyone in the faerie ring now grabs a partner and all the pairs jump the besom in turn. They may make wishes as they jump, either shouting them out or wishing them silently.

Once everyone has jumped the besom the King and Queen of Cobwebs take each other's hands and are the last couple to jump the broomstick.

If anyone in the faerie ring writes poetry or has a favourite poem they would like to read out, fitting to this seasonal tide, then now would be the time.

Now, as an exception in honour of the mischief and chaos, the May King and Queen bless the cakes and mead. The Priest and Priestess of Elphame then say farewell to the Faerie King and Queen. They also perform the remainder of the tasks necessary to close down the ritual and banish the circle.

The ritual ends with the faerie ring sitting together holding hands in a circle and closing down their chakras. The Priestess of Elphame leads a short grounding exercise for everyone and then the Beltaine feast begins.

The King and Queen of Elphame

The candles on the altar for this rite should be green, as should the altar cloth. You will also need dried or fresh rose petals and acorns. This is the ritual for the faerie ring to honour the Faerie King and Queen and explore their relationship and the magical possibilities this alliance can bring. This rite can take place on any phase of the moon apart from the three days of the dark moon.

Once everything has been prepared for the rite, the ring holds hands. The Priest and Priestess of Elphame ask everyone to forget the world outside and visualize the Faerie King and Queen.

Beginning with the Priestess of Elphame, a kiss is sent deosil around the circle with a 'Blessed Be'. The Priestess then asks everyone to sit down and open their chakras.

The remainder of the preparing and casting the circle follows as before until raising the power, when 'treading the spiral' would be the most effective method for the energy of this rite.

Once the power has been raised the Priestess of Elphame asks everyone to make themselves comfortable for meditation in the faerie circle. Once everyone has taken their places, the Priest of Elphame recites a poem:

Priest of Elphame: 'Queen of Elfland, in your place between,
this world of ours is quite unseen.
With your fey King behind the shroud,
wave your wand and part the cloud.
Let us meet you in this circle fey,
An elfin journey we'll tread today.
Blessed Be.'

*The Priestess of Elphame now takes everyone
through a pathworking:*

'You see a beautiful woodland, a lush place in late summer. The weather is warm and it is raining very lightly. The sound of the gentle rain on the leaves entrances you for a moment and takes your mind to a place of solace and calm. After a while the rain stops and a warm mist rises from the woodland floor. Through the mist emerge the Faerie King and Queen. They are of course your chosen personal mentors and appear to you now as they have always done. They are walking together, as if in a faerie court, holding hands. They hold them up, as if in a stately procession.

Suddenly they both glance over to where you are standing and for a brief moment, their poise is interrupted. They both smile and wink at you, as if acknowledging that you are part of a secret that they share too. They then continue their formal walk through the woods. They pass through what looks like a wall of fine mist and disappear. You follow and enter the mist too. Walking through the mist is a sensation strangely like gliding.

You are greeted by a land in sunset. Elphame lies before you. A meadow of golden wheat sways in the evening breeze and the Faerie King and Queen stand in the centre of the field as if waiting for you. You wade through the tall wheat until you reach them. They stand in a circular clearing and a wall of wheat encloses you all. Around them are dancing many hundred sylph faeries, as if they are magnetized by the fey monarchs. Before the King and Queen on the earth lies a beautiful crystal wand. This is for you to use while in Faerie Land.

You may pick up the wand and as you do so it tingles and sparkles in your hands. The wand is a symbol of your own power, but it is amplified in Faerie Land and you have the use of it while you're here.

Faerie Queen: "Take the wand
of crystal clear.
Wave your hand,
for dreams so dear."

Faerie King: "Of one wish you have to make,
for yourself or others' sake.
If there are any answers you do seek,
With the wand you may take a peek."

The Faerie King and Queen both kiss you on the cheeks. Use the wand to ask a question, personal or otherwise, and a picture should be revealed. Like a dream, it will not be straightforward and will need unravelling. I will leave you for a few moments to spend your time with the wand.

When you have completed your task, return the wand to your Faerie King and Queen. Remember that it will always be there if you need it, in the care of your fey King and Queen. Walk back through the wall of mist whence you came and back out into the late summer woodland.

You may now open your eyes when you are ready to come back.'

After making sure that everyone has returned safely from the meditation, the Priestess of Elphame asks the ring to sit in a circle and hold hands. Now everyone who wishes to share their pathworking experience can do so in turn. This often turns into a long and in-depth discussion time and the seekers can help one another with the meanings of the symbolism in their experiences.

The Priest and Priestess of Elphame then lead a part of the rite in honour of the Faerie King and Queen. The Queen of Cobwebs is asked to light a silver candle on the altar for the Faerie Queen. Once this has been done a faerie seeker volunteer creates a circle of rose petals on the floor, encompassing all those in the ring. The King

of Cobwebs lights a second candle on the altar for the Faerie King. A second seeker volunteer creates a second circle, adjacent to the rose petal one, this time made of acorns or similar woodland fruit.

Priestess of Elphame: 'We call our Faerie Queen,
to our hearts. We sincerely mean,
to honour her in petals fair,
and draw her here with every care.
Blessed Be.'

Priest of Elphame: 'Faerie King, our work you bless,
with your Queen in gossamer dress.
We meet you in this circle of light,
of love and mirth here tonight.
Blessed Be.'

Once the pathworking is complete, if anyone in the ring has a spell they need the whole group to help them with, then now would be a good time.

After this the cakes and mead are blessed and shared by the Priestess of Elphame, who then says farewell to the Faerie King and Queen and closes down the circle.

The ritual ends with the faerie ring holding hands in a circle and closing down their chakras. The Priestess of Elphame leads a short grounding exercise and then the ritual feast begins.

The Psychic Hangover

When you have visited Faerie Land, you have entered another place, another state, and your whole being has been affected by the shift. For this reason, some people take some time to adjust when a ritual ends. This is especially evident if you have performed an invoking of the Faerie King or Queen.

This 'psychic hangover' can last up to three days and simply means that you are not totally grounded in everyday reality. It can be likened to a very mild astral bender. Even if you closed your chakras down thoroughly after the ritual and feasted, Faerie Land can still be connected to you by a celestial ribbon. A psychic hangover can make you feel dreamy and unfocused and your thoughts will often still be in the ritual. This is the key to avoiding a hangover: being strict with your thoughts and trying to focus on mundane things. This should start the moment you leave the ritual.

If you are the sort of person who is prone to psychic hangovers, shut the lid on your imagination for a while. With some sensitive people, even thinking about the events of the previous ritual can pop open your chakras again. I have found that on some occasions, writing up my ritual has opened my chakras again and fuelled a psychic hangover.

So if you wake up a little dreamy and swimmy-headed, don't fuel that hangover with thoughts of the ritual, but be disciplined about the day ahead and focus your mind on something as far away from Faerie Land as possible. You will find that once you have knocked the dreamy feeling on the head with mundane thoughts, it will not float back your way until your next faerie circle.

Faeriecraft rituals should be an enjoyable part of your life and should weave in and out of it without any uncomfortable feelings. However, for rituals to be a regular part of your being, they should not cross over into everyday life. Faerie Land is only meant to be visited for a short while at a time, otherwise consequences, however mild, can drift into everyday life. As a Faerie Priest or Priestess, you are responsible for your own life and for maintaining the balance between walking in Faerie Land and your own world. It may take a little practice at first, but a psychic hangover or two, like the alcoholic kind, will make you a lot wiser.

11

Under the Faerie Tree
How to Create a Faeriecraft Wedding, Baby Naming and Other Rites of Passage

'The iron tongue of midnight hath told twelve;
Lovers, to bed; 'tis almost fairy time.'

WILLIAM SHAKESPEARE,
A MIDSUMMER NIGHT'S DREAM

The Icing on the Faerie Cake

This chapter is really the icing on the cake for the faerie seeker who wishes to embrace the faerie pathway in all areas of their life.

The rites of passage celebrations I have given here are similar to ones that I have written for myself and my family. Even guests of differing religious backgrounds or no faith at all have found them enjoyable and fascinating and asked lots of interested questions afterwards about what we believe in. When inviting non-faerie seekers to a family celebration, remember that everyone has some experience of faeries, if only from books from their childhood, and so everyone has some sort of 'way in' to understanding the rite.

When a ceremony like a faerie wedding, baby naming or passing is held, it is usual for a Priest or Priestess of Elphame to officiate, as they are seen as representatives of the Faerie King and Queen. Also, more practically, they have experience of leading rituals in the faerie ring and so can transfer their skills to other faerie celebrations. This is not to say that any Faerie Priest or Priestess cannot officiate if requested to do so and if they feel confident in this role.

The Naming of a Faerie Childe

This rite is a mixture of the baby-naming rites I used for our children Morgan and Tam Lin. I feel I have taken the best bits from both celebrations to bring you a beautiful rite on which to base the naming of your own baby. This ritual is your template only and you may introduce roles and poetry with personal significance as and when required.

A naming ceremony is usually a family occasion, and for this reason the actual rite needs to be lightened to suit the nature of the event. For example, there is no need for everyone to open their chakras, as you will not be doing any psychic work. For this chapter I will assume for simplicity's sake that a Priestess of Elphame is officiating at the celebration and a baby girl is being named.

The ideal is to hold the ceremony outside, but if you are working indoors then you will have to adapt yourselves to the space available. With Tam Lin's naming, we were extremely fortunate to be able to hire a stone circle for a few hours, the Rollright Stones in Oxfordshire, and there was plenty of space for all our guests, but such opportunities are not always available and you will have to make the best use of your own locality.

Prior to the ceremony godparents should have been chosen. Our daughter Morgan's godmother calls herself a 'faerie godmother'. This is such a lovely description that I have used it in this ceremony.

The Priestess of Elphame stands in the centre of the circle, with the faerie childe in her parents' arms and the faerie godparents-to-be by their side. The guests stand around the outside of the circle. For this occasion, you may like to mark the circle out with rose petals or similar material.

Priestess of Elphame: 'We are met in this gathering to ask the blessing of the Faerie King and Queen on............., the daughter of............ and............., so that she may grow in beauty and strength, health and wisdom.

There are many paths to follow in this life and everyone must find their own. Therefore we do not wish to bind this faerie childe to any one path while she is still too young to choose. Instead we ask the Faerie King and Queen to bless, protect and walk with her through her years of childhood and when she is grown up she will know which pathway she should tread. But for now she is a faerie childe.'

The Priestess of Elphame now consecrates and casts the faerie circle. Once she has blessed the salt and water, a little is sprinkled on the faerie childe, parents, faerie godparents and anyone else who is assisting in the ceremony.

Once the circle has been cast, the Priestess of Elphame makes a doorway with her wand at the north-east point and welcomes the guests to the naming each with a kiss and 'Blessed Be'. Once all the guests are in the circle and standing around the perimeter, the Priestess of Elphame closes the doorway and seals it with her wand.

*Priestess of Elphame: 'Can ………… and …………
please bring their fairy childe …………forward.'*

The parents bring the baby to the Priestess, who anoints her on the crown of her head with sweet oil.

Priestess of Elphame: 'I anoint you with oil in the name of the faerie King and Queen and bless you the name …………'

Priestess of Elphame: 'Guardians of the East,
sylphs of the whispering wind,
bless you with inspiration and communication,
the joy of the stars, the breath of life.'

The Priestess of Elphame fans the baby with a large feather (one from a peacock or swan is ideal).

Priestess of Elphame: 'Guardians of the South,
salamanders of the flickering fire.

bless you with passion and warmth,
the joy of the sun, the spark of life.'

The Priestess of Elphame lights a candle on the altar for the faerie childe.

Priestess of Elphame: 'Guardians of the West,
undines of the shimmering water,
bless you with dreams and moon-imbued thoughts,
the joy of a waterfall, the mysteries of life.'

The Priestess of Elphame consecrates the faerie childe lightly with water.

Priestess of Elphame: 'Guardians of the North,
gnomes of the fertile earth,
bless you with understanding and sensibility,
the joy of the earth, the gifts of the body.'

The Priestess of Elphame strokes the baby with a bouquet of flowers or sweet herbs.
Priestess of Elphame: 'Are there two who will stand as faerie godparents to ....?'
The two godparents come forward and the Priestess of Elphame now takes the faerie childe in her arms to face the godparents.
Priestess of Elphame: 'Do you both, faerie god-mother and godfather to ...., promise to be a

special friend to her throughout her childhood, to guide her whenever she needs you and, in agreement with her parents, watch over her and love her as if she were your own family, until she is ready to tread her own pathway in life?'

The faerie godparents answer in their own words.

Priestess of Elphame: 'May the kingdom of the faeries, the moon and the stars, the sun and divine love shine in life for ...., this faerie childe. We wish you a magical life, dear ....

'Now I ask any of our guests to come forward if they would like to bestow a wish upon this faerie childe to take her forward in life.'

(During Tam Lin's naming, lots of guests seemed to really enjoy this time of the ceremony. The idea comes from the fairytale Sleeping Beauty. As long as the thirteenth fairy doesn't turn up to give her bad wish, it should all be fine!)

When everyone who wants to has given the baby their wishes then the Priestess of Elphame walks over to the north-east point once more. She opens a doorway in the circle with her wand and gestures to the guests to filter out of the circle.

Once the guests have left the faerie circle, the Priestess of Elphame closes the circle. The feast of course then begins, hopefully with merriment and dancing too in honour of the faeries' most favourite pastime.

A Wedding Made in Elphame

If you are planning a faerie wedding in advance, the most favourable time in the tides of the year is Beltaine, 30 April, a time of fertility and fecundity. A faerie wedding can of course happen at any time of the year and a natural setting is always lovely too.

The circle and altar should be decorated with flowers and it is customary for the bride to wear flowers in her hair as well. A note of preparation: the cakes and mead are blessed before the ceremony begins and not at the usual time.

The Priestess of Elphame stands in the centre of the circle and the guests stand around the outside.

Priestess of Elphame: 'The Faerie King and Queen bring together today, by the sun, the moon, and eternal love, our bride and groom .... and ....'

The Priestess of Elphame now consecrates and casts the faerie circle. Once she has blessed the salt and water, a little is sprinkled on the bride and groom and anyone else who is assisting in the ceremony.

Once the circle has been cast, the Priestess of Elphame makes a doorway with her wand at the northeast point and welcomes the guests into the circle with a kiss each and 'Blessed Be'. The last ones to enter are the bride and groom and their attendants. The bride and groom enter together and hold hands. They come to stand before the altar, which in this rite is in the centre of the faerie circle.

Once all the guests are in the circle and standing around the perimeter, the Priestess of Elphame closes the doorway and seals it with her wand.

Priestess of Elphame: 'To this faerie wedding we bring all the elements that be: the sylphs of air bring the power of the intellect, the salamanders of fire bring the power of passion, the undines of water bring love and desire, the gnomes of the earth bring the power of natural law.'

The Priestess of Elphame now asks the bride and groom to raise their clasped hands, the bride's right hand and the groom's left. She ties their two hands together with a red ribbon, a symbol of their unity.

Priestess of Elphame: 'Now say after me. [To the groom] In the presence of the Faerie King and Queen, I .... take .... to my heart and my soul, at the rising of the moon and the fullness of the sun, to love and honour one another; our bodies, hearts and spirits to be bound as one. For death will not part us, as our souls shall live on together in all eternity.'

(This last sentence is optional and it should be discussed beforehand whether the couple want a soul commitment.)

The Priestess of Elphame now repeats the same to the bride.

Once both the bride and groom have repeated the above to each another, the ceremony can continue.

Priestess of Elphame: 'All here now bear witness that .... and .... have been joined together under natural law. Let this be so by all the faerie kingdom and their elemental beings, the moon, the stars and the sun. A wedding made in Elphame is now duly blessed. Would .... and .... please partake of this mead as a pledge of your love and eat this wedding cake as a pledge of your marriage under natural law.'

The Priestess of Elphame takes up the chalice and offers the bride and groom a sip. She then takes two small portions of the cake and offers them to the bride and groom.

The Priestess of Elphame then unties the red ribbon round the bride and groom's hands. The groom and bride are then passed the wedding rings by their attendants. They exchange rings. These would have been previously placed on the faerie altar on a small velvet cushion or similar. The bride and groom now kiss.

Priestess of Elphame: 'Behold the chariot of the
Fairy Queen! Celestial coursers
paw the unyielding air; Their filmy pennons
at her word they furl,
And stop obedient to the reins of light;
These the Queen of spells drew in,
She spread a charm around the spot,

And leaning graceful from the ethereal car,
Long did she gaze, and silently,
Upon the slumbering maid.'

Percy Bysshe Shelley, *Queen Mab*

Priestess of Elphame: 'May the Faerie King and Queen bless them in their life together. May it be magical, beautiful and strong. So mote it be!'

The Priestess of Elphame then takes the faerie besom and lays it down on the ground before the bride and groom. They jump over it hand in hand.

She then opens a doorway at the north-east point with her wand. She gestures for the guests to filter out of the circle. The bride and groom lead out first, followed by their attendants and guests.

The Priestess of Elphame then closes the circle. The wedding feast can now begin and don't forget to leave a little of the wedding cake out for the fey!

The Faeries Are Invited to Tea: A Birthday Celebration

This really is one of my favourite faerie celebrations. It is not a ritual, but a celebration and meditation. It can be celebrated on your own or with a group of like-minded friends or family.

First the room needs to be prepared. The altar, as always, is the focus. For your birthday choose your favourite flowers, if they are in season, or you may prefer to decorate your altar in foliage and berries rather than flowers. The choice is yours.

The birthday cake is also an important part of the celebration and should be placed on the altar. A home-baked cake is great because you can decorate it with your own design. If this is not possible, then you can buy a plain celebration cake and decorate it yourself, choosing a faerie theme. If you are reasonably artistic, then faerie themes such as mermaids, winged sylphs, butterflies and gnomes can be painted onto royal icing with liquid icing sugar using a fine paintbrush. If you are not artistically inclined, then a local baker will always be able to decorate a cake for you according to your own ideas.

Once you have set the scene, then you can begin your birthday celebration.

First of all you are going to close your eyes. Say a small prayer in your own words, asking the Faerie King and Queen to bring you protection and blessings upon your birthday.

Now imagine a circle of white light surrounding you and your altar, creating a celestial perimeter around you. Visualize this circle of white light whizzing deosil. See it whirring around so fast that it hums, like a cat

*purring. Once you have created your circle and it feels
right, invite the faeries to tea:*

'Once upon a time,
on this special day of mine,
a rainbow spanned from heaven to Earth,
a bridge of light to bring my birth.
A childe of the heavens I used to be,
now of the Earth I'm Blessed Be.
To celebrate my birth here today
I wish to make merry in the faerie way.
So sylphs of air, salamanders of flame,
come together and dance from Elphame.
Undines of water and gnomes of earth,
welcome to my circle, on the day of my birth.
Birthday cake and mead so sweet,
I share with you to drink and eat.
So, faeries, now I invite you to tea,
To celebrate my birthday and Blessed Be.'

*Once you have invited the faeries, imagine that your
altar is glowing with golden shimmering light. Imagine
that your circle is full of faeries, all come to celebrate your
birthday with you. Your circle is abundant with the fey,
bringing a beautiful energy of peace and love.*

*Now is the time for you to enter into your birthday
meditation. This is the purpose of enjoyment only!
Relax and take your time. You have the faeries at your
birthday party, so it's bound to be magical.*

Imagine that you are in a woodland clearing. The time of year is of course your birthday, so it is up to you to see the trees and the woodland surroundings in the season appropriate to the time of your birth.

The clearing is covered in the most beautiful green moss, which also peppers the bark of the trees around you. This creates a lush woodland carpet for you to sit on. Take a seat in the middle of the clearing, in the faerie ring, and feel comfortable there. It is a magical place, on the cusp of Elphame, on the edge of both worlds.

Beside you is a picnic basket. Open the lid and peer inside. It's all for you and your faerie guests. There are miniature cups and saucers and little plates. Set these all out on the moss before you for your guests. There is also a usual-sized cup and saucer and plate for you to use. Now set out the cakes on the plates and fill the cups with mead.

Once you have done this, close your eyes and listen to the stillness within the woodland clearing. A white mist begins to fill the circle. You open your eyes to see the mist, a glistening, shimmering mist of magical happenings to come. In it you begin to see the outlines of tiny forms emerging into the clearing. It is hard to see them at first, but after a while the mist separates and you can see them quivering in spectrums of light. The beautiful lights slowly transform into solid faerie beings. Before you are a gnome, a winged sylph, a water undine and a sparkly salamander.

Suddenly you look down to find that you are holding a crystal wand, tipped with a star from the night's sky. You look up to see the owner of the wand standing at the edge of the clearing. She smiles and gestures to the wand, as if to tell you that it is meant for you. After a few moments, you see her image fade into the glistening white mist. She has vanished from sight: the Faerie Queen.

Now each of the elemental faeries in turn comes up to you and presents you with a gift. You give them each their mead and a cake and say 'Blessed Be'. When they give you their gifts, they may speak to you or they may just present the birthday gift. These gifts are not transferable to our world and can only be used on the astral planes. However, you can visit the woodland clearing whenever you need to and use one of the gifts, which will stay untouched on the moss. The faerie gifts may also be symbolic and if you are unsure about them, you are permitted to ask the giver their meaning. For example a crystal ball may be the gift of foresight or a wand may be symbolic of a sharpened intellect. This part of the meditation is between you and the faerie folk.

Once you have received your birthday gifts and shared the cake and mead with the faerie beings, they simply shimmer into the white mist once more and you are left alone in the mossy circle.

Through the mist you suddenly see a faint image of your faerie queen. She blows you a magical kiss, which you receive like a kiss upon your heart. Then, as quickly as she appeared, she too vanishes into the mist.

When you are ready it is time to open your eyes.
Cut the cake on the altar and leave a piece on the plate
for the faeries. Now raise your chalice of mead and say
a toast to the fey.

'Faerie Queen, out of shimmering mist,
I bless you for your faerie guests.
A taste of Elphame was my wish,
To share my birthday I have been blessed.'

Take a sip of your mead and then place the chalice
on the altar. If you are celebrating with friends, now
would be a good time to share the cake and mead. Don't
forget to make a wish when you blow out your candles
– even this simple act is candle magic.

Now visualize the white light that forms your circle
and see it dissolving. Let the light fall into the ground
and fade completely away until there is nothing left.
Perform a simple grounding exercise, as you have medi-
tated, and then, in faerie style, have a fabulous birthday
party celebration!

A Coming-of-Age Celebration

Reaching the age of independence and being accountable in your own right is a joyous occasion. In magical terms, 18 is a very significant age and brings all sorts of spiritual openings to the faerie seeker. This is because most faerie ring groups (and this goes for witches' covens too) will not admit anyone under the age of 18. This is because developing spiritually and psychically usually demands a mature personality who has at least got over the worst of all the turmoils of growing up. Developing magically opens psychological doors which children do not always have the maturity or emotional scope to cope with.

Some faerie rings or covens do admit minors under 18, but these are few and far between. What often happens with these groups is they have family-centred rites and celebrations especially written for the children and their parents. The magical energies are toned down and deities with powerful energies are not invoked. If an adult ritual is to be worked, it is done in the evening when the children are tucked up in bed. I have worked in a family group and these need parents who are willing to sacrifice their own spiritual development for a while. Family faerie rings do, however, have the wonderful benefit of seeing the children who have grown up in the ring coming of age and becoming apart of the adult rites if they choose.

There is nothing to stop someone under 18 working as a solitary, but this should *always* be done with adult guidance at hand.

I have written this ritual to celebrate the coming of age of a girl who has grown up in a faerie ring. It may also be worked by a number of solitary faerie seekers who have come together to celebrate a fellow faerie seeker coming of age. As there are no formal initiations in faeriecraft, this is a magical celebration rather than an initiation.

The room or outdoor ritual space should be decorated in honour of the celebrant. You could use flowers and foliage in season and even balloons and ribbons. The choice is yours, but whatever you do, really make an effort, for the faeries love a celebration. If possible, the ritual space can be prepared before the guest of honour enters, so that it is a surprise.

Once the altar and ritual space have been prepared, all the members of the faerie ring stand in a circle and hold hands apart from the celebrant and the Queen of Cobwebs. These stand outside the circle and may watch the proceedings until it is time for them to enter.

The circle is cast as usual by the Priest and Priestess of Elphame. The appropriate power raising would be a joyous dancing of the spiral dance. Once the power has been raised, the Priestess of Elphame takes up her wand and draws a door in the north-east of the circle for the celebrant and the Queen of Cobwebs to enter.

Priestess of Elphame: 'Those who enter into our ring,
honour the Faerie Queen and King.
Faerie seeker, we welcome you,
Your time has come, so enter do.'

The Queen of Cobwebs brings the young celebrant into the circle and she is received with a kiss and 'Blessed Be' first by the Priest and Priestess of Elphame and then the rest of the faerie ring.

Everyone holds hands in a circle and the group begins to 'pulse' deosil. This is a method of bringing a group's energy in tune and is also lots of fun – in our group it usually ends up in giggles. The Priest or Priestess of Elphame begins this energy exercise. Starting with their left hand, they squeeze the hand of the person standing to the left of them and then quickly let go. Once the person to the left has received the squeeze, they immediately pass it on to the person next to them and so on until it completes a circuit around the circle. This finishes at the Priest or Priestess of Elphame once more, then it starts all over again. This circle of squeezes can go on for as long as the Priestess of Elphame wishes and it usually defies all logic, with the pulsing whizzing around the circle at an incredible rate. Each squeeze of the hand should be accompanied by a burst of positive energy to the person on the left.

Once the pulsing is finished, the celebrant is asked to stand in the centre of the circle. The Queen of Cobwebs places a faerie crown upon her head as a gift to her. The Priestess of Elphame gives her the gift of a magical tool. This could be a wand or chalice, for example, for her to keep.

The King and Queen of Cobwebs:
'A faerie childe you stepped upon the Elphame path,
a faerie seeker you now tread the green-lit way.
The place between the worlds,
you may now enter in your own right,
to learn faerie magic and the ways of the earth.
Your Faerie King and Queen now take your hand,
and you may pass into Faerie Land.
Blessed Be.'

The Priest and Priestess of Elphame:
'The faerie circle, our place of power,
reveals the secrets to those we seek.
To Elphame we travel through the oaken door,
and now you are invited today and more.
Blessed Be.'

*The young celebrant may now read out a poem that
she has previously chosen and prepared. After this the
Priest and Priestess of Elphame will anoint her with
sweet oil upon her third eye.*

Priest and Priestess of Elphame:
'The place of magical sight to see the fey,
We bless you with this today.'

*Now comes the fun part, as everyone in the ring
softly chants the name of the celebrant and takes part in
decorating her. This can turn into a very giggly affair. It
should of course be carried out with the utmost respect*

for the celebrant and she should be warned beforehand that it will take place. Temporary transfer tattoos can be applied, and her face and body can be decorated with body paint with pictures of stars, moon, faeries, toadstools: go wherever your imagination takes you! Confetti can be thrown over the celebrant and her hair plaited in many coloured ribbons. Paint her feet and toenails, put body glitter on her hands and feet and adorn her with flowers. Really make her feel special and a centre of the ritual.

Priestess of Elphame: '.........., the Faerie King and Queen honour you as we have done tonight, as a being of the heavens and earth, a fey-blessed one, ready to enter Elphame. We invite you to walk your own faerie pathway, along the green-lit path.'

Everyone now takes a partner and makes an arch-way in a line, so that the celebrant may walk under-neath from one end to the other, emerging at the altar.

Celebrant: 'In this stardust body I now make my own way, a faerie seeker from this day. Blessed Be.'

The Priest and Priestess of Elphame now bless the cakes and mead and offer them first to the celebrant. The circle is then closed as usual and a feast and party should ensue.

Family Celebrations

The whole family can celebrate the faeries in very simple ways, without bringing ritual into it, from a very early age. In our family we have a small centrepiece in the middle of our dinner table. The children like to decorate this and we leave it up to them as their 'thing' to honour the faeries. It changes naturally with the seasons and can be a collection of crystals, feathers or conkers, but always with a candle in the middle to be lit at every mealtime.

Special decorations can be found at significant times, such as full moons, sabbats and family occasions. The fey are not pious and would not want you to celebrate them in an overtly religious way. Faeries are fun and they naturally inhabit a child's imagination, so if you want to incorporate simple family faerie celebrations, then it's easily done by lighting a candle at mealtimes and telling a story or reading a poem.

A Passing to the Otherworlds

I have only ever been to one pagan funeral, but it was a truly magical and profound celebration of the person's life as a priestess. It was also a very personal tribute, and I think that with a faith such as faeriecraft, you do have the freedom and scope to create a farewell ceremony that honours your loved one in a very personal way. For that reason I am only going to give here the outlines of a farewell ceremony. It is for you to bring the personal touches, such as poems, tributes, songs and pieces of music.

It is most likely that this ceremony will be held at a crematorium. The limitations of the venue have been borne in mind with the ceremony given here. However, if the person is being buried in a natural place, you have the freedom to alter it to suit your needs.

For simplicity I have assigned the Priestess of Elphame to officiate over the ceremony and considered the deceased to be a woman. As always, this is only a template for your own inspiration.

The venue should be adorned with abundant flowers. If a simple archway of flowers and foliage can be created, so much the better, as this is symbolic of the passage from this world to the next. The casket should be placed before the archway of flowers. Once the guests have assembled, the Priestess begins.

Priestess of Elphame: 'Today we meet to remember and say our farewell to .... who walked the pathway of life following faeriecraft. For this reason, the ceremony today includes the faeries who touched her life.

Dearest Faerie King and Queen,
elfin monarchs who are unseen,
touch our hearts here today
in your special faerie way.

East bears air, the wind soars,
South frees fire, the flame roars.

West springs water as it flows,
North cradles earth; a seed grows.

Of all the elements far and near,
witness, bless and be present here.
So mote it be.

*We meet not only to say farewell and remember, but
also to free .... from the earthly life into the care
of the Faerie King and Queen, so that she may rest
until she is born again. Knowing that she moves to a
place of beauty and love, a place that she loved herself,
I hope will bring comfort to all those who remember
and love her.*

*For a few moments I invite you all to silently
remember .... in the way that you knew her.'*

(Silent remembrance)

*After the silent remembrance would be a good point
for any pre-arranged tributes from friends or family to
be read out.*

*Priestess of Elphame: 'Now we return .... to
the elements whence she came.*

Dear Faerie Queen,
dissolve the dream.
Let her journey begin,
by your Faerie King.
Faerie Queen, take her hand.

Take her now to your land.
Through the misty veil she goes,
in her silent and blessed repose.'

*This is the time when the coffin is taken through
the archway of flowers and through the curtains. The
Priestess says:*

'Blessed be, elements four,
air, fire, water, earth, you came.
Depart through the faerie door,
proceed to your realms with faerie name.
So mote it be'.

*A closing poem may be recited here or music played
as the guests file out and dedicate their parting wishes.*

Afterword

The Faerie King and Queen gave this book to me as a
gift. Writing *Faeriecraft* has been one of the most intense,
creative, spiritually engaging and uplifting times in my life
and a magical experience in itself. I entrust this book to you
and hope that you emerge inspired and enlivened, as I have
been, to tread the faerie pathway to Elphame.

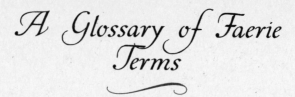

A Glossary of Faerie Terms

Here I have listed words that are used in all magical practices, as well as terms that are uniquely faerie. This is because faeriecraft is a spiritual pathway belonging to a wider family of pagan paths. You may well come across many of the terms listed below when reading further books.

anima   The feminine expression of a man's unconscious.

animus   The masculine expression of a woman's unconscious.

athame   A black-handled knife traditionally used by a witch to cast circles and invoke energies, etc. This is not a tool that is used in faeriecraft because it is made from metal.

aura   The body's own energy field, comprised of different colours, indicating well-being, mood and level of spiritual attainment.

Book of Elfin   The faerie seeker's own handwritten book recording their rituals, spells, etc. and serving as a magical diary. Peculiar to the path of faeriecraft.

Book of Shadows   The book that each witch keeps to record their rituals, spells, etc. This book is copied by hand from their initiator.

censer   Usually a metal container with a perforated lid, used specifically for burning natural incense on charcoal discs.

chakras   The body's energy centres. There are seven main points. These can be used in faeriecraft for focusing energy from the Earth or from the heavens on particular magical tasks.

chalice   A goblet which is placed upon the faerie altar. In faeriecraft it can be made from wood, glass or silver and is used for the ritual partaking of mead.

charge   A poem, verse or speech given by the faerie seeker who is invoking the Faerie King or Queen during a ritual.

Cobwebs (King and Queen of)   The male and female assistants to the leaders of the faerie ring. Their main duty is sweeping the faerie circle and being its gatekeepers or guardians.

coven   A magical working group of three or more witches, usually up to a maximum of 13.

craft   A term used to describe witchcraft.

Daoine Sidhe   The Irish faerie people ruled by King Finvarra and his Faerie Queen Oonagh. They were once

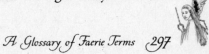

the Tuatha de Danaan, but became the small faerie folk of the Daoine Sidhe after being driven out of their hollow hills by the invading Celtic Milesians.

dark moon   The three days of the moon's cycle when the moon is hidden. Generally speaking, it is best to avoid working magic at this time, as it is a time of magical rest.

deosil   The direction of the sun. In the northern hemisphere this is clockwise.

Dianic coven   A magical working group which is exclusively female and works with goddess deities. Named after the moon goddess Diana.

elements   The essential components to faeriecraft and magic: air, fire, water, earth and ether.

elf/elfin   Words interchangeable with *faerie*.

Elfland/Elphame   Other names for Faerie Land. Elphame is the Scottish name.

faerie altar   A table covered in a cloth and adorned with a faerie seeker's magical tools, faerie offerings and ornaments. Used as a focus for communicating with the fey.

faerie besom   A magical tool similar to a traditional witch's broomstick. In faeriecraft they are always decorated to the owner's taste and their primary function is to sweep negative and everyday energies from the faerie circle.

faerie childe   A child born into a family which practises faeriecraft.

faerie circle   The magic circle cast by the faerie seeker to practise magic or enact celebrations, a place which exists between the two worlds.

Faerie Land   The place where all the kingdoms of the fey dwell, a place of magic and enchantment.

faerielore   All that is known about faeries, their land and their society.

faerie ring   A group of three people or more who meet to practise faeriecraft.

faerie seeker   An individual who practises faeriecraft.

faerie temptress/tempter   The Faerie Priestess and Priest of old.

fey   An interchangeable word for *faerie*.

gnome   An earth elemental.

invocation   The drawing of the essence of either the Faerie King or Queen into the faerie circle and into the being of the Faerie Priest or Priestess.

magic   Bringing about change in our physical lives by focused will, using esoteric knowledge and training.

new moon   The last day of the dark moon phase. The best time to practise magic for new projects or ventures.

Old Religion   The religious ways of our pagan ancestors; the seasonal observances also celebrated by the fey.

Otherworld   Another name for Faerie Land.

pagan   An individual who follows a pre-Christian spiritual pathway such as a druid, shaman, witch, etc. The word used to refer to a country-dweller, i.e., someone who followed the seasonal tides. Faeriecraft is also a pagan pathway.

pathworking   A guided meditation following a journey of enlightenment.

pentacle   A five-pointed star enclosed by a circle. Also a disc made of wood, symbolizing the earth, used on the faerie altar.

pentagram   A five-pointed star not enclosed by a circle; like the pentacle, it symbolizes the five elements.

Priest/Priestess of Elphame   Male/female faerie seekers who have founded their own Faerie Ring, look after its day-to-day running, take the focal roles in rituals and officiate over rites of passage.

rath   A faerie mound, also known as a hollow hill, surrounded by a circular field and sacred to the faerie race, who are believed to dwell there.

ritual   A set procedure or celebration. In faeriecraft rituals are used to celebrate sabbats or moon phases or to work magic, or a combination of these.

rune   In faeriecraft, a chant used for magical purposes.

sabbats   The eight seasonal tides of the year, celebrated as festivals.

salamander   A fire elemental.

scrying   A method of divination involving a bowl of water or a dark mirror. The faerie seeker uses this method to see images either by their third eye or physical eyes.

solitary   A faerie seeker who magically works alone.

spellcraft   The use of magical spells within a framework of knowledge and training to bring about a specific result.

staff   A long piece of wood, around the height of its owner; a magical tool, interchangeable with the wand as the focus of the faerie seeker's magical will and intent.

sylph   An air elemental.

thurible   Another word for a censer, used to burn natural incense on charcoal discs.

Tuatha de Danaan   The race originally known as the 'people of the Goddess Danu' who were driven out by the Celtic Milesians and became the small and invisible faerie race. They now reside within the hollow hills of Ireland.

Underworld In much folklore the same as Faerie Land, also sometimes known as the Land of the Dead, where passed souls dwell.

undine A water elemental.

visualization Using your imagination to see images in your mind's eye and to experience them with all your senses. A magical tool.

wand A piece of wood or crystal, usually the length of a faerie seeker's forearm from the elbow to the tips of the fingers. A magical tool used in ritual as a focus of the seeker's magical will and intent.

waning moon The phase of the moon when it is decreasing from a full moon. The best time to practise any magic on a banishing theme.

waxing moon The phase of the moon when it is increasing to a full moon. The best time to practise magic of an attracting and creating nature.

wicca A pagan mystery religion akin to witchcraft with a less traditional thread.

widdershins 'Against the sun'; in the northern hemisphere, this is an anti-clockwise movement.

witch A man or woman who practises witchcraft.

Bibliography

Here are works which I have referred to or quoted from and which may inspire you on your faerie path.

Katherine Briggs, *A Book of Fairies*, Penguin Books, London, 1997

Vivianne Crowley, *Wicca: The Old Religion in the New Age*, The Aquarian Press, Wellingborough, 1989

Alma Daniel, Timothy Wyllie and Andrew Ramer, *Ask your Angels*, Piatkus Books, London, 1995

'The Faeries', anonymous seventeenth-century English poem in Celia Haddon, *The Faerie Kingdom*, Simon and Schuster, London, 1998

Pierre Dubois, *The Great Encyclopaedia of Faeries*, Simon and Schuster, New York, 1996

Janet and Stewart Farrar, *Eight Sabbats for Witches*, Robert Hale, London, 1981

Janet and Stewart Farrar, *The Witches' Goddess*, Phoenix

Publishing Inc., Washington, 1987

Steve Fox, 'The Faerie Ring', unpublished

Anna Franklin, *The Illustrated Encyclopaedia of Fairies*, Vega, London, 2002

Brian Froud and Alan Lee, *Faeries*, Pavilion, London, 1995

Brian Froud, *Good Faeries/Bad Faeries*, Pavilion, London, 2000

Brian Froud and Terry Jones, *Lady Cottington's Pressed Fairy Book*, Pavilion, London, 2000

Jack Gale, *The Goddess Holda*, Hagal, London, 1998

Jack Gale, *Goddesses, Guardians and Groves*, Capall Bann Publishing, Chieveley, 1996

Alicen Geddes-Ward, 'The Kiss of Two Worlds', unpublished

Robert Graves, *The White Goddess*, Faber and Faber, London, 1961

Rosemary Ellen Guiley, *Fairy Magic*, Element Books, London, 2004

Marie Heaney, *The Names upon the Harp*, Faber and Faber, London, 2000

Andrew Lang, 'The Terrible Head', in Joanne Rippin (ed.), *Fairies: An Anthology of Verse and Prose*, Lorenz Books, London, 1996

Claire Nahmad, *Fairy Spells*, Souvenir Press/Past Times, London, 1997

Christine O'Brien (ed.), *Fairies: An Anthology of Verse and Prose*, Lorenz Books, London, 1996

William Shakespeare, 'A Midsummer Night's Dream' in *The Works of William Shakespeare*, Frederick Warne and Co., London, n.d.

Percy Bysshe Shelley, *Queen Mab*, in Karen Sullivan, *The Little Book of Faeries*, Brockhampton Press, London, 1996

Kisma K. Stepanich, *Faery Wicca: Book One*, Llewellyn, St. Paul, Minnesota, 1994

Simon Steward, 'Oberon's Apparell', 1635, in Karen Sullivan, *The Little Book of Faeries*, Brockhampton Press, London, 1996

Doreen Valiente, *An ABC of Witchcraft Past and Present*, Robert Hale, London, 1973

Doreen Virtue, *Earth Angels*, Hay House, Inc., Carlsbad, 2002

Doreen Virtue, *Archangels and Ascended Masters*, Hay House, Inc., Carlsbad, 2003

Doreen Virtue, *Angel Medicine*, Hay House, Inc., Carlsbad, 2004

Kate West, *The Real Witches' Coven*, Element Books, London, 2003

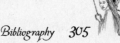

Dominic Williams, 'The Faerie Temptress', unpublished

Recommended Reading

I have only included books here that I have read myself and know to be informative. Some of them are just for fun, but they ignite the imagination too, an equally honourable passageway into Faerie Land along with knowledge. At the end of the list I have included just a few works of fiction, as I do not feel that this list would be complete without adding them.

Faerie Information Books

Katherine Briggs, *A Book of Fairies*, Penguin Books, London, 1997

Joe Cooper, *The Case of the Cottingley Fairies*, Pocket Books, London, 1990

Pierre Dubois, *The Great Encyclopaedia of Faeries*, Simon and Schuster, New York, 1996

Anna Franklin, *The Illustrated Encyclopaedia of Fairies*, Vega, London, 2002

Brian Froud, *Good Faeries/Bad Faeries*, Pavilion, London, 2000

Brian Froud and Jessica Macbeth, *The Faeries' Oracle*, Fireside, New York, 2000

Rosemary Ellen Guiley, *Fairy Magic*, Element Books, London, 2004

Paul Hawken, *The Magic of Findhorn*, Fontana/Collins, Glasgow, 1976

Sheila Jeffries, *How to Meet Fairies*, Capall Bann Publishing, Milverton, Somerset, 2001

Edain McCoy, *The Witch's Guide to Faery Folk*, Llewellyn, St. Paul, Minnesota, 1996

Claire Nahmad, *Fairy Spells*, Souvenir Press/Past Times, London, 1997

Marc Potts, *The Mythology of the Mermaid and her Kin*, Capall Bann Publishing, Milverton, Somerset, 2000

Serena Roney-Dougal, *The Faery Faith*, Green Magic, London, 2003

Doreen Virtue, *Healing with the Fairies*, Hay House, Inc., Carlsbad, 2001

Sage Weston, *A Year in the Life of a Faery Witch*, Capall Bann Publishing, Milverton, Somerset, 2001

Amber Wolfe, *Elemental Power*, Llewellyn, St. Paul, Minnesota, 1998

Books for Fun and Inspiration

Ann Dahlgren/Douglas Foulke, *A Fairy's Child*, Harry N. Abrams, Inc., New York, 2002

David Ellwand, *Fairie-ality*, Walker Books, London, 2002

Brian Froud and Terry Jones, *Lady Cottington's Pressed Fairy Book*, Pavilion, London, 2000

Pagan/Wiccan Information

Vivianne Crowley, *Wicca: The Old Religion in the New Age*, The Aquarian Press, Wellingborough, 1989

Glennie Kindred, *The Earth's Cycle of Celebration*, Earthkind, Oxford, 1991

Starhawk, *The Spiral Dance*, HarperSanFrancisco, New York, 1989

Angels and Deities

Doreen Virtue, *Earth Angels*, Hay House, Inc., Carlsbad, 2002

Doreen Virtue, *Archangels and Ascended Masters*, Hay House, Inc., Carlsbad, 2003

Doreen Virtue, *Angel Medicine*, Hay House, Inc., Carlsbad, 2004

Works of Fiction

Holly Black, *Tithe: A Modern Faerie Tale*, Simon and Schuster, New York, 2002

Wendy Froud and Terri Windling, *A Midsummer Night's Faery Tale*, Simon and Schuster, New York, 1999

Wendy Froud and Terri Windling, *The Winter Child*, Simon and Schuster, New York, 2002

Deborah Wright, *The Rebel Fairy*, Time Warner Paperbacks, London, 2002

DVDs

John Walker, *The Fairy Faith*, Wellspring Media, New York, 2000

Resources

www.faeriefellowship.com A website founded by the authors to provide a point of contact for all those wishing to follow faeriecraft and get in touch with others who follow the same pathway. It features an online newsletter and notice-board for faerie seekers to use.

www.faeriecraft.co.uk The authors' website and companion to this book, featuring information on forthcoming faerie workshops across the UK and residential workshops in Orkney, Scotland, up-and-coming faerie projects run by the authors, web links and beautiful faerie imagery.

www.magicwings.co.uk Beautiful site of handmade wings, tiaras, wands, etc. for the dedicated faerie seeker to order.

www.witchcraft.org This is the website of the Children of Artemis organization and primarily a focal point for wiccans and witches, but it has many aspects that would benefit the faerie seeker. Annual events across the UK, also a fantastic magazine, *Witchcraft and Wicca*, a high-quality and well-respected publication.

www.worldoffroud.com The website of Brian and Wendy Froud, faerie artist and author; faerie dolls.

www.gothicangel.co.uk Featuring the artwork of artist Steve Fox; outstanding faerie images.

www.faeriefestival.net Information about faerie festivals in the US organized by Spoutwood Farm, Glen Rock.

www.faerieworlds.com Information about the Faerieworlds Festival held annually in Arizona, USA, organized by Imaginosis and Woodland Productions.

About the Authors

Alicen and Neil Geddes-Ward are a writer and artist respectively and frequently work collaboratively as a creative team.

Alicen works as a writer and Faerie Priestess and travels extensively throughout the UK giving workshops and lectures on faeriecraft. She regularly contributes articles to magazines and has also had numerous plays performed and toured internationally in the theatre with faerie/esoteric themes. She has appeared on TV and radio and been described as 'the UK's leading exponent on faeries'.

Pagan and visionary artist Neil Geddes-Ward is one of the founder members of the prestigious British Visionary Artists' Group which attracts esteemed artists from all over the UK to exhibit and publish their work collectively. Neil's artwork is influenced by dreams, psychic and astral experiences and the pagan imagery of the British landscape. He has appeared on TV and radio and his work has appeared in books and magazines and on CDs in the UK, US and Australia. He has exhibited widely throughout the UK, including Glastonbury. His work sells internationally as prints and cards and is both celebrated and highly collectable.

During the writing of this book, Alicen and Neil moved to Orkney, the ancient group of islands off the north coast of Scotland and home to many faerie legends and mermaids, where they hope to gather inspiration for further faerie books and works of art.

To contact the authors and see more of Neil's beautiful artwork, please visit the following websites:

www.faeriecraft.co.uk
www.neilgeddesward.com
www.faeriefellowship.com

To see more of Neil's artwork and find out more about faeries, visit the Orkney Faerie Museum and Gallery founded and run by the authors on the Isle of Westray, Orkney, Scotland. Please visit the authors' website for more details.

If you would like to contact the authors, please write to the following address:

Alicen and Neil Geddes-Ward
PO Box 1
Orkney
KW17 2WY

email: neil@geddesward.co.uk or
alicen@geddesward.co.uk

Index

Kings and Queens are listed under their given names in this index, as well as having a sub-entry under 'Kings, Faerie' or 'Queens, Faerie'. However, where the word 'King' or 'Queen' forms part of another title, it is listed directly (e.g., the King and Queen of Elphame ritual is listed under 'K'). Main entries are indicated in **bold** and illustrations in *italics*.